LIFE, DEATH, *and* CATHOLIC MEDICAL CHOICES

50 QUESTIONS *From the* PEWS

KEVIN O'NEIL, CSsR
AND PETER BLACK, STD

D1316907

Liguori

Imprimi Potest: Harry Grile, CSsR
Provincial, Denver Province, The Redemptorists

Published by Liguori Publications
Liguori, Missouri 63057
To order, call 800-325-9521, or visit liguori.org.

Imprimatur: "In accordance with c. 827, permission to publish has been granted on March 1, 2011, by the Most Reverend Robert J. Hermann, Auxiliary Bishop Emeritus of St. Louis, Archdiocese of St. Louis. Permission to publish is an indication that nothing contrary to Church teaching is contained in this work. It does not imply any endorsement of the opinions expressed in the publication; nor is any liability assumed by this permission."

Library of Congress Cataloging-in-Publication Data

O'Neil, Kevin, 1955-
Life, death, and Catholic medical choices : 50 questions from the pews / by Kevin O'Neil and Peter Black.—1st ed.
     p. cm.
  Includes bibliographical references and index.
  ISBN 978-0-7648-1953-7 (alk. paper)
  1. Medicine—Religious aspects—Catholic Church. 2. Medical ethics—Religious aspects—Catholic Church. 3. Catholic Church—Doctrines. I. Black, Peter, 1954-
II. Title.
  R725.56.B563 2011
  174.2—dc22

                                                                              2011001461

Scripture citations are taken from the *New Revised Standard Version* of the Bible, copyright 1989 by the Division of Christian Education of the National Council of Churches of Christ in the USA. All rights reserved. Used with permission.

Liguori Publications, a nonprofit corporation, is an apostolate of the Redemptorists. To learn more about the Redemptorists, visit Redemptorists.com.

Printed in the United States of America
19 18 17 16 15   6 5 4 3 2

First edition

CONTENTS

We dedicate this book to two extraordinarily faith-filled women

whom we remember with gratitude and love:

Sister Joan Flynn, RSM (1923-2010), aunt of Peter Black,

and

Margaret A. O'Neil (1921-2010), mother of Kevin O'Neil.

May they rest in peace.

INTRODUCTION

Questions raised in this book touch on some of the most profound moments of joy, fear, anger, and sorrow in our lives. Joy at the news of a long-awaited pregnancy, at an optimistic prognosis for an illness, at the news that an organ donor has been found, and even bittersweet joy as a loved one accepts her approaching death with courage and peace. Fear may accompany the diagnosis of an illness, the report that a treatment is not working, or at the news that death is near. Sadness arises at our own or a loved one's suffering, at the news of infertility, at death. Anger may surface in all these instances of fear and suffering, and even in our relationship with God.

Responses to these questions will never address adequately all the thoughts, emotions, and feelings that accompany important decisions that we make. They attempt, however, to offer information, principles, and the reasoning that is at work in Catholic Church teaching in response to many questions that surface at the beginning of life, in moments of life "in between," and at the end of life.

Browsing through these responses, readers will note time and again that emphasis is placed on certain fundamental concepts that form the core of the Catholic Church's teaching and promote our embracing responsibly our own lives and those of our brothers and sisters. Attuning our minds to these issues will help us to respond even to questions not asked or answered here.

Before addressing these important concepts, we must say a word about the most basic criterion in Catholic teaching for judging right and wrong action: authentic human good. Blessed Pope John Paul II wrote: "Acting is morally good when the choices of freedom are *in conformity with man's true good* and thus express the voluntary ordering of the person toward his ultimate end: God himself, the supreme good in whom man finds his full and perfect happiness" (*The Splendor of Truth*, #72). Notice that it is when human beings are prized that one stands right before God. The fundamental concepts that we briefly review here concern precisely "man's true good" or authentic human good.

First is the dignity of the person as one made in the image and likeness of God. We possess dignity simply because we are, not because of our intelligence, our independence, our health, our contribution to society, our faith, or any other reason other than that we exist. The Church's teaching that human life is to be respected from conception to natural death is grounded in this profound respect for each human life as an image and likeness of God, whether that life be the tiniest embryo, a homeless person needing medical care, a person in a persistent vegetative state, or a frail elderly person awaiting death. All are equal in dignity. To live and to die with dignity is to live and to die as one made in the image and likeness of God.

A second point is respect due to human life itself. Our tradition recognizes human life as a fundamental gift from God, without which no other gifts may be enjoyed. Unless we are alive we cannot experience the joy of friendship, family, music, sports, or any other thing that makes life enjoyable. The primary gift that comes with life, however, is the possibility of a relationship with the same God who offers us life. A recurring theme in Catholic teaching is that we ought to always respect our physical lives and those of others, but not as ends in themselves. We are destined for eternal life with God. This spiritual end of our lives is primary and holds a place of utmost importance with regard to all judgments that we make throughout our lives. We ought neither cling to our physical lives as if they are all we have nor should we disrespect our own or another's life and hasten its diminishment.

The gift of life comes to us in a particular body, our body. This is a third point to keep in mind. The Catholic tradition holds great respect for the body, linked to our belief in the goodness of all creation but also to Jesus' Incarnation, his taking on our human flesh and nature. For this reason, the Church teaches that we are really a union of body and soul. It would be even better to speak of an ensouled body or an embodied soul since there is no division between the two. Frequently what affects the body touches the soul and vice versa. Our experience confirms this point. Physical sickness affects our spirit; sometimes our spirits are so low that we feel aches and pains in our bodies. People don't say, "My liver has cancer," but "I have cancer." We are a union of body and soul.

A fourth point touches on the human person as relational. Right from conception we are in relationship with others. Many of the questions in this book arise from the bonds of relationship: Who makes decisions for a loved one? May I donate my body to science? Can I force someone I love to seek medical treatment? We live as social beings, and the judgments that we make affect not just us but those around us. Good moral decisions are never made in isolation from or without concern for others.

A fifth point to consider in the Christian tradition is its particular perspective on human suffering. We should be clear that suffering is not good in itself, and we have a long tradition of trying to ease suffering and to walk with people as they experience it. Suffering is not something that can be cured or taken away (like physical pain); it attacks the human spirit and sometimes requires a human journey to work our way through it. While the Church encourages us to overcome suffering, it also recognizes that suffering can have a positive value in our lives. A common experience of those who suffer is a feeling of isolation, of being disconnected from themselves and others. Faced with suffering, the greatest temptation is to close in upon oneself and to stop loving others. In this case, suffering destroys us as images of God because it gets in the way of our loving others. On the other hand, when suffering is endured with courage, is made bearable with the support and expertise of others, and does not block our love, it can take on a new meaning in the light of the sufferings of Christ, who himself did not stop loving in his suffering. Christians should be in solidarity with those who suffer, especially the sick and the dying, for suffering can deepen the faith and love of us all. "This mysterious vocation of yours to suffering is a vocation to love for God the Father of Mercy, and for other brothers and sisters. Only Christ's cross can illuminate our weak intelligence and give it a glimpse of the deep meaning of the human and Christian fruitfulness of suffering" (Pope John Paul II, December 20, 1981).

A final introductory point concerns our understanding of health itself. A Vatican document titled the *Charter for Health Care Workers* states: "The term and concept of health embraces all that pertains to prevention, diagnosis, treatment and rehabilitation for greater equilibrium and the physical, psychic and spiritual well-being of the person" (*Charter for Health Care Workers*, §9). Although we frequently associate health with the body, this broader understanding of health is very important and helps put some of the responses in perspective.

As we have already stated, one's spiritual well-being is primary. One should not be surprised, then, that one's relationship with God might play an important role in making decisions about life. Someone might make medical choices based on psychological well-being, concerned about responsibilities to loved ones and being reconciled with others. This broader definition of health underscores the personal and unique context in which judgments about life are made. Although Church teaching offers both general and particular guidance on many issues, final judgments ought to be made always by individuals with a well-formed conscience, in light of the particular circumstances of their lives.

Chapter 1

INTRODUCTION TO QUESTIONS ABOUT THE BEGINNING OF LIFE

Jesus once compared the kingdom of God to a mustard seed, the tiniest of seeds. Yet it grows to become a bush large enough for the birds of the air to come to nest in it (Matthew 13:31–32; Luke 13:18–19). Perhaps most of us have never seen a mustard seed but are familiar with acorns. Standing before a fully grown oak tree, we may find it difficult to believe that it began as something as small as an acorn, which we can hold easily in the palm of our hand. Human beings, too, come from the tiniest material, an egg and sperm. Once they are joined in conception, however, the journey of growth begins. Standing before a fully grown human being, or even holding a newborn baby, we may find it difficult to believe that this human life came from a single cell that could hardly be seen in the palm of our hand, yet it is true. Provided with the proper environment and care, the tiniest new human being will develop in the womb, be born, and continue to develop until natural death.

As miraculous as each new human life is, we find ourselves at times in moral dilemmas precisely around issues at the beginning of life. Someone may be heartbroken that she cannot conceive a child while someone else doesn't feel ready to receive a child into the world. News of advances in science that seem to promise "miracles" for people suffering from diseases require the destruction of new human beings for their research and therapy. Couples who experience infertility discover that some options for having a child present ethical problems themselves.

Frequently in these early life matters, we come back time and again to the unity of body and soul, and the danger that comes when we fail to take this into consideration together. New life, while described by some as "a clump of cells," is a new human being; both the matter, the "body," and the soul are important. The experience of infertility in the body brings sadness in the soul. Certain attempts to resolve fertility issues separate spouses' gifts of their bodies, their whole selves, to one another in efforts to bear a child.

Embracing life and respecting the dignity of all human beings from the very beginning is a consistent teaching of the Catholic community. Its teaching that a new human life begins at conception is based on sound scientific evidence, not on an arbitrary judgment of the magisterium of the Church and theologians. In the face of challenges at the beginning of life, we are reminded constantly of the equal dignity of all human beings and our obligation to respect the dignity of one another.

The questions and responses that follow relate to some instances at the beginning of life. We trust that they will be informative but also encourage us to consider how we might embrace life at its beginning and to stand with those who are suffering and seeking support in the challenges that they face.

1. When does a living human being or a person begin?

This seemingly simple question is of utmost importance in bioethics and, in the view of some, difficult to answer. There are really three aspects that must be considered in answering this question: scientific, philosophical, and moral. The question concerns when human life begins, when it is deemed a person, and an unspoken question as to when and why we should respect a person.

Regarding the scientific perspective, Church teaching states clearly that a new human being begins living at conception, that is, when a sperm and egg are joined and become a separate unique organism. This new life is distinct from the lives of the parents or the ones who provided the eggs and sperms, in the case of artificial reproductive technologies. The key point is that this new life now possesses its own genetic individuality and, given the proper environment, will continue to grow. Church teaching does not arise from religious conviction but from a philosophical interpretation of scientific information.

From a philosophical perspective, Church teaching holds that a unique individual human being is a person. The technical philosophical definition of a person is an individual substance of a rational nature.

The moral question is why each individual must be respected and protected. It is because of the dignity of each human life. Each new human life passes through several stages of development but, according to Church teaching, these stages do not constitute different levels of moral status or value. The same kind of respect is due to developing human life from the time of conception through to the end of human life.

This last point about the respect that is due to human life from the beginning is related to the question about when a person begins. In the Catholic moral tradition, persons have moral status and possess rights, the most basic of which is the right to life. In our relationships with persons, we ought to protect them and not endanger their lives, much less deprive them unjustly of life itself. Church teaching states that human life is to be treated "as a person" from the time of conception. As we said, in the Catholic tradition, a person has been defined as an individual, rational creature. One of the difficulties that the Church recognizes in speaking of personhood right from the beginning of human life is that it is possible for embryos to split to become identical twins and also to come together again after splitting. The question is then raised as to whether we had an individual or two individuals. This is a relatively infrequent occurrence, but it poses a question that needs to be answered. Some people object that an embryo is not capable of reasoning at this stage. Yet the embryo is the first stage of ongoing development. Nothing will be added to the developing life to give it the power of reason. It simply needs to develop. The Church's answer about questions of personhood even at this early stage is based on two points: probability and risk.

It is probable that this new being is a person; to directly kill such a being is to risk killing a person. To deliberately take such a risk shows that one is willing to kill a person. The Church affirms then that all human beings are to be treated as persons from conception through natural death.

2. What does the Church teach about abortion?

It is important to describe abortion accurately in order to respond to this question. Pope John Paul II described it in his encyclical letter, The Gospel of Life, in this way: A "procured abortion is the deliberate and direct killing, by whatever means it is carried out, of a human being in the initial phase of his or her existence, extending from conception to birth" (#58).

Several words are particularly important in this description. He speaks of a "procured" abortion because there are times when tragedy strikes and pregnancies end unexpectedly and painfully because of unfortunate physical circumstances independent of anyone's actions or intentions. Procured abortions ordinarily require the assistance of medical personnel to intentionally end the developing human life.

Secondly, John Paul speaks of abortion as "deliberate and direct killing." So the persons seeking the abortion and those who carry it out fully intend to end the life of the child and choose to do so freely. "Direct" means that the death of the new life is the result of a specific action performed to bring about its destruction. There are times when human life is lost at this stage because of other actions by medical personnel who perform surgical interventions that are aimed at curing a pathology and who do not intend to carry out abortions. For example, a pregnant woman who is diagnosed with cancer of the uterus may undergo surgery to remove the cancerous uterus knowing that doing so will cause the death of the fetus. In these cases the death of the child is neither deliberate nor direct. In fact, if the child were viable and able to live outside the womb, every effort would be made to save its life. The death of the child in this instance does not meet the description of abortion as deliberate and direct killing.

Returning to the initial statement: Abortion is understood as that which is procured and entails the direct and deliberate killing of a human being. Why is this morally wrong and is never justified? Why is this the case?

The Church holds for the sacredness and inviolability of all life, but particularly innocent human life precisely because of the dignity of each human life created in the image and likeness of God. To deprive a human being of life is to take away the most fundamental human good that we have. Without life we cannot enjoy any other human good, such as relationships with others, the spiritual life, and so forth. Church teaching adds another argument against the taking of innocent human life in an instance such as abortion. That is, God is the author of life; we are stewards of the gift of life. We ought not reject or abuse a gift of God. Even though persons may find themselves in painful and very difficult situations, deliberately and directly taking innocent life is an immoral response. Every effort must be made to assist women with difficult and even unwanted pregnancies to know that they are not alone and will not be left alone in bearing and raising their children.

---

3. Is abortion ever morally justifiable, for example, in cases of rape, incest, or in order to save the life of the mother? Is the "morning after" pill OK to use after a rape?

Understanding abortion as we have described it earlier, that is, the deliberate and direct taking of innocent human life, standard Catholic moral theology could not justify abortion in any case, including those listed here.

The desire to end a pregnancy that is the result of an act of violence and power as in rape and incest is understandable. The child of that pregnancy would be a constant reminder to the mother, during pregnancy and during life, of the act of rape or incest that produced the child. However, the child himself or herself is an innocent party in these situations. The Church would suggest offering all means of psychological, spiritual, and material support to enable a woman to deal with trauma and to bear the child and to decide what the best way forward would be in this tragic situation.

A further question is raised regarding the use of what is often called "emergency contraception" in cases of rape. Church teaching is clear that one may never administer medicine to prevent the implantation of a fertilized ovum. In such a case, medicine would really be an abortifacient, effectively preventing new life from implanting in the uterus. The fifth edition (2009) of Ethical and Religious Directives for Catholic Health Care Services, approved by the United States Conference of Catholic Bishops, states: "If, after appropriate testing, there is no evidence that conception has occurred already, [a victim of rape] may be treated with medications that would prevent ovulation, sperm capacitation, or fertilization. It is not permissible, however, to initiate or to recommend treatments that have as their purpose or direct effect the removal, destruction, or interference with the implantation of a fertilized ovum" (Directive #36).

---

4. Is it acceptable for a Catholic healthcare professional to be employed by a hospital that performs abortions, provided she has nothing to do with these procedures?

The question raises an important issue regarding any intentional involvement in wrongdoing. Application of this material extends beyond this example to many other situations in our lives. The case presented here is fairly straightforward. In fact, a person may work in a hospital that performs abortions, provided that she has nothing to do with the procedures. Because performing abortions is only one part of what the hospital does, a person may work there contributing his or her expertise to other areas of healthcare. If the circumstances were different, and the place of employment was a clinic dedicated to terminating pregnancies through abortion, it would be morally wrong to work there.

The reasoning in this response is guided by the principle of cooperation. It asserts that we may never intentionally cooperate approvingly in the morally wrong action of another person. To consent to help another and to approve of his morally wrong action is termed formal cooperation. Cooperating with another reluctantly, disapproving of what he is doing, is called material cooperation. One may never cooperate formally in another's wrongdoing because, in doing so, one also performs an immoral action, knowingly and willingly. Some material cooperation may be morally justified, but not if a person's cooperation is necessary for an immoral action to occur.

5. Why is the Church against stem cell research?

The Church is not opposed to all stem cell research. It is one particular kind of stem cell research, embryonic, that it judges to be immoral. The reason for this position is tied to the dignity of all human life and that a living human being is to be respected as a person from the time of conception. How does this reasoning apply here?

In embryonic stem cell research, the early embryo, sometimes only four or five days old, is destroyed as researchers take cells out of the core or nucleus of the embryo. These are stem cells, called embryonic stem cells because they are from a destroyed embryo, which researchers hope to learn how to reprogram into the various cells of the human body. However, because this process destroys the developing, living human being, whom we are required to treat as a person, the Church judges this method of stem cell research as wrong.

Many have judged the Church's position as callous, seemingly insensitive to people suffering from a variety of diseases that scientists hope may be alleviated or cured through embryonic stem cell therapies. The Church, while very much sensitive to the suffering of all human life, judges that the destruction of any innocent human life for whatever good motives and goals is never justified. Again, for this reason, embryonic stem cell research is judged to be morally wrong.

In addition to embryonic stem cells are adult stem cells, found in various parts of the human body, especially bone marrow, blood and fatty tissue. Interestingly, one of the most productive resources for adult stem cells is the umbilical cord blood remaining after birth. The Church actively supports adult stem cell research and would welcome other techniques for obtaining stem cells that do not entail the destruction of human embryos. In fact, in 2010 the Vatican announced a grant of nearly $3 million to help fund adult stem cell research. Various reports speak of the success of adult stem cell therapies in treating a variety of injuries and diseases.

The critical difference between these two types of stem cell research is that human life is destroyed in embryonic stem cell research. It is not in adult stem cell research.

6. What does the Church teach about medical responses to infertility? Are fertility drugs morally acceptable?

One of the most natural desires of married couples is to want to have children. Not infrequently many couples suffer greatly because of their inability to have a child. Infertility, described as the inability to conceive a child after trying to do so for more than a year, seems, according to statistics, to be rising in its occurrence. The Church recognizes the suffering of such couples but, as in other comparable instances, calls upon the faithful and those in the field of science and medicine to respond to this suffering in a way that is consistent with authentic human good.

A simple guide that Church teaching offers is the following. Technological methods or medicine that assist the natural means of conception through sexual intercourse may be morally acceptable. Those methods that replace sexual intercourse in bringing about new life are not morally sound. Why does the Church offer this principle?

Marriage is a special kind of self-giving, and this self-giving is expressed in and through the body, that is through bodily intercourse. A technological instrument that replaces bodily intercourse cannot be the means of a fully human personal, mutual self giving of man and woman. The language of technology is quantified calculation: the language of love is expressed in words and bodily intercourse.

Further, when conception is separated from this act of love of spouses, as occurs in many artificial reproductive technologies, there is a danger that it may harm the relationship of the spouses and also treat new life as a commodity and not as a gift. A further concern in Church teaching is that God's role as author of life would be lost sight of when the miracle of each life is treated like a product in the hands of scientists and medical professionals. We will address some of these methods of artificial reproduction shortly.

Where do fertility drugs fit into this picture? Church teaching encourages the use of anything that can resolve the problem of fertility, such as hormonal treatments and various surgical interventions, as long as these treatments assist and do not replace the natural process of reproduction through sexual intercourse. In such a case, they are morally acceptable and consistent with authentic human good.

---

7. Does the Church have teachings regarding particular methods of artificial reproductive technology, such as *in vitro* fertilization, surrogate motherhood, and the like?

The same reasoning and principle from Church teaching stated in the previous question apply here as well. Simply put, any artificial reproductive technologies that replace conception by means of sexual intercourse between spouses are judged to be morally wrong. Church teaching has addressed a variety of means of reproduction in this manner: Artificial insemination by one's husband (AIH), artificial insemination by a donor (AID), *in vitro* fertilization, cloning, and surrogate motherhood.

In each of these cases, the process of conception occurs in a manner other than through sexual intercourse. In two instances, (AID and surrogate motherhood) a third party is involved in the process, donating sperm or bearing the pregnancy and then relinquishing the child to the one who will raise him or her. There may be other instances of third-party involvement, such as the use of donor egg and donor sperm for the *in vitro* fertilization process.

Church teaching comes back to the fundamental concern for the new life that will come into existence, the relationship of the spouses and the place of God in bringing about new life. Some reproductive technologies may have a greater impact on the relationship of spouses than others, for example, when a third party is involved.

8. My cousin "adopted" an embryo and now has a beautiful little boy. Does the Church approve of embryo adoption?

The issue of "embryo adoption" arose because artificial reproductive technologies often require that more eggs be fertilized than it is wise to transfer to a woman's uterus. As a result, clinics frequently freeze these embryos for later use or, with the permission of the donors, donate them for research purposes. As indicated in an earlier question, the Church opposes this kind of manipulation and creation of new human life as not respecting the dignity of human life. Yet, there exist thousands of embryos that are destined for destruction or for experimentation. One asks if it is morally licit to "adopt" one or more of these embryos as a way to rescue a new human life from destruction.

In a document called "The Dignity of the Person," the Church recognized the good intentions of people who would want to give these embryos a chance to develop fully as human beings. Nonetheless, the Church notes that the methods used to carry the child to term are morally objectionable because of reasons mentioned earlier: that the child is not conceived as a result of sexual intercourse of spouses, the danger of a third party or more in the process of bringing forth new life, and the ongoing fear of treating new life like a product.

While applying teaching on reproductive technologies to this particular situation, one can almost hear the frustration of the teaching office of the Church as it states that these "abandoned embryos" are *"a situation of injustice which in fact cannot be resolved"* (#19). Nonetheless, we are reminded that every child who comes into this world, regardless of the moral failures of those responsible, is ultimately a gift from God.

9. Does the Church promote adoption as a response to infertility and, if so, why?

The Church does indeed promote adoption, but not solely as a response to infertility. In documents that deal with reproductive technologies and infertility, Church teaching raises the question of adoption as a possible alternative way that a couple might direct their generosity and desire to be life-giving through children. While recognizing the suffering prompted by infertility, the Church also sees the great need of children throughout the world who, for one reason or another, have not been able to live with their biological parents.

The call to adopt and to care for children in need throughout the world, however, is addressed to all believers who are able to help. The theological foundation for reaching out to adopt children is linked to our being brothers and sisters in Christ and that we are called to be stewards of the lives of one another. In some instances, people may feel called to care for needy children of the world by adopting them and bringing them into a new family to develop and grow.

In some situations, perhaps Christians could show extraordinary love by "adopting" a child or a family of children by supporting them in their own country through assistance to relatives who could not otherwise look after the child. This is obviously not like raising your own child in your own home; but think of what this might do for a child in his own home country. In other words, one of the key principles that should underlie the care of orphans is "what is best for the child."

10. Should adopted children or children born of artificial reproductive technologies know who their biological parents are?

Arguments may be made in favor of and against adopted children or children born of donor parents knowing their biological origins. It appears more and more that adoption agencies encourage knowledge of biological parents over closed adoptions, where this information is not known by the child or adopting parents. There are many issues here that are packed emotionally, such as why someone was relinquished for adoption, fear by adopting parents that this new information could compromise their relationship with their child, perhaps fear on the part of biological parents that they will be asked to be involved in a relationship against their wishes. Many other issues surface and merit consideration, but they fall outside our competency and focus here.

An argument to be made in favor of open adoption and disclosure of information about one's biological parents touches on the focus of our concerns here, one's health, and in particular we concentrate on the physical and psychological dimensions of health. Today we realize that challenges to our health come not just from bacteria and viruses that invade our system from outside ourselves, but also from within, that is, from genetic predispositions to heart disease, diabetes, and other disorders that could compromise our well-being. Although genetic testing is done to some degree in procedures where donor sperm or eggs are used for reproduction, there is currently no practical substitute for access to the medical history of one's blood family. This information becomes more critical when persons are of an age to marry and to bear their own children. They might want to know as much information as possible to act responsibly in bearing and raising children.

Although anonymity may be preferred by a biological mother who has borne a child whom she does not feel equipped to nurture through life, the anonymity and whole practice of donating sperm and egg and virtually relinquishing all responsibility for offspring is very problematic morally. Although many parents have been overjoyed at the birth of children born through these procedures, one must challenge the disconnection between the child's biological roots and the rest of his life. There may come a time when he will want to know who his biological mother or father is. Yet the practice of donating egg and sperm is structured according to commercial models and for the most part to disconnect intentionally biological parents from their offspring.

---

11. I read about a couple who had a baby by means of artificial reproductive technologies in order to provide a perfect match of bone marrow for their sick daughter. Does Church teaching approve of this way to cure a disease in a child?

There are many aspects to this question, some related to the Church's opposition to embryonic stem cell research and to some artificial reproductive technologies. A chief concern is the dignity of each human life and that human beings must not be used as a means to an end. While sympathetic to the sufferings of those who are suffering and even dying, the Church holds that the means used to respond to such tragedy must respect human dignity and life in all areas.

When parents try to conceive a child who is a perfect match for their sick child, certain technologies must be used that offend human dignity. First of all, conception would take place in a laboratory, not through sexual intercourse. If an ongoing danger is that new human life might be treated as a product of our own making, this fear is more relevant in the present case. In fact, after embryos are created, only the one(s) that match perfectly the sick sibling would be considered for transfer to the mother's womb. In that selection process, other embryos would either be frozen or discarded precisely because they do not fit the wishes and hopes of the parents and medical personnel.

Further, there is potential harm to the child who is born. Although she might rightly be called a hero for helping and perhaps even saving her sibling, the child might wonder whether she was ever wanted for herself.

While media reports bring happy news of successful birth of children who are perfect matches for their sick brother or sister and while the Church encourages us to welcome human life in whatever way it comes to us, Church teaching would still consider this practice morally wrong because of the harm and potential harm done to one or more human lives while seeking a benefit for another one.

C h a p t e r 2

INTRODUCTION TO QUESTIONS ABOUT LIFE "IN BETWEEN"

A physician friend of ours begins a course to medical students by reminding them that they are all dying. It is unlikely that they anticipate such an opening line from a doctor/professor. One of the reasons for taking this approach, however, is to encourage medical students to see themselves as not so different from the people whom they will treat in their practice. While they may be relatively healthy and view their patients as sick, they are encouraged, rather, to see themselves and their patients at different stages of the same journey, some closer to death than others.

Sometimes retreat directors have asked people making a retreat to write their own obituary. It may sound like a morbid exercise, but its purpose is to push people to consider how they would like to be remembered. It also encourages them to ask themselves, "How ought I live now so as to have this obituary be true when I am gone?"

In both these cases, people are offered a context or a perspective on life. They are to use their imaginations to see their reality in new ways, perhaps life-changing ways. As we reflect on some questions that touch on life "in between," that is, in between conception and natural death, what ought to be the perspective that colors the way we live and make decisions about matters of health? We suggest that it is our relational nature that ought to predominate, that we never lose sight of ourselves as people in a relationship with God, with others, and with ourselves. How do we live and make important decisions in our lives so as to harmonize these relationships, to live with integrity?

Sometimes our relationship with God is strained as we face medical challenges in our lives, wondering where God is. Other times we might wonder how best to receive the gift of life from God and care for it properly, perhaps even wondering if we are distrusting God when we seek medical help.

Living "in between" is always living in relationship with others as well. How do we attend best to those entrusted to our care? As our medical and scientific knowledge increases, information that we learn about our own genetic makeup may be important for others. Some people not only care for their own bodies but want to help others even in their suffering or after their death. So, they consider organ donation or donating their body to science. Perhaps the basic question is: "How do we live in this 'in between' time concerned for the life and health of others and responding to their needs as we are able?"

Finally, how do we live in a way that is true to ourselves as people of dignity, created in the image and likeness of God? Being good stewards of our own health is the proper response to the gift of life from God.

Being healthy means, above all, harmonizing our relationship with God, with others, and with ourselves. That entails attention to the physical, psychological, and spiritual aspects of our lives as people who live in relationship and are destined for fullness of life forever with God. Keeping this perspective may guide us as important issues surface in our lives and keep us on track to be healthy in the truest sense.

12. Is there a right to healthcare?

AND

13. What kind of obligation do I have as a Catholic to use my resources to help with the purchase of medicine for my brother? His insurance won't cover the costs, and he's on a fixed income. I'm feeling guilty.

We combined these two questions because the first question might tend to lead to an abstract discussion about rights and duties while the second question puts a human face on the question: a person's brother. As so many of the questions of this book arise from the experience of people and their loved ones, we should attempt to keep the sickness and suffering, indeed the faces, of real people in mind as we reflect on our response.

For a variety of reasons and for centuries, the Church avoided using human rights language. It altered this course, however, in 1963 with Blessed Pope John XXIII's encyclical letter, Peace on Earth. He said that people have a right to live and a right to the "means necessary for the proper development of life" (#11). This text serves as a foundation for the United States Conference of Catholic Bishops' speaking of a right to "basic" or "adequate healthcare" in their Ethical and Religious Directives for Catholic Health Care Services. What is not clear in Church teaching is who has the duty to ensure that people enjoy this right. In some cases the state has taken this responsibility, but this need not be the case. The condition of millions of our brothers and sisters in Christ whom we have never met, however, urges us to action on their behalf.

Regarding the particular case of one's brother, does he have a right to the medicine and do we have a duty to provide funds for it? This question is difficult to answer because of the need for more information. What is the brother's prognosis? Is he taking care of himself responsibly? Does he have an ordinary or an extraordinary obligation to take this medicine? What do you feel capable of doing morally without placing yourself and others in your care at risk?

Not knowing the responses to these questions, we would find it difficult to say "yes" or "no." Whatever one's ability to respond in this case, one's relationship with one's brother should be marked by compassion and a sincere desire and will to help in whatever way is morally reasonable.

14. Does the Church have a position on cosmetic surgery?

For the sake of clarity, we understand cosmetic surgery to be a medical intervention that is purely optional and not medically necessary. These medical treatments are not required to maintain or to restore the physical health of a patient. We are not considering here plastic surgeries in response to physical injury due to a fire or trauma or things of that sort. It is not possible to give a single response about all types of cosmetic surgery, and the Church has no explicit teaching on the matter as of this writing. Perhaps some general principles will help to guide our thinking in specific cases.

Our tradition holds such respect for the human body that it insists that any harm done to the body must not be outweighed by risks and be justified by a greater good. A principle that helped to form the moral response regarding surgery is the principle of totality, where harm may come to a part of an organism for the good of the whole. A dramatic example of the application of this principle is the amputation of a gangrenous limb. The removal of a healthy leg, for example, would clearly be an atrocity. However, when the leg endangers the whole person, the tradition justifies amputation for the good of the whole.

When we approach the question of cosmetic surgery, we must ask what the goal of the surgery is and whether it justifies the kind of intervention that will occur. Face lifts, "nose jobs," "tummy tucks," and so forth are elective surgeries usually pursued because persons are not happy with the way that they look. While there may be certain instances where people are so distraught over these matters that cosmetic surgery would help them to attain some peace and comfort with themselves, often these surgeries are motivated by concerns arising from vanity. Even when these feelings are present, one might ask reasonably whether more profound issues about acceptance of self should be addressed, rather than resorting to a fixing of one's physical appearance. Keeping in mind that care for the body always takes place in the larger context of our relationship with God, one ought ask if and how this particular cosmetic surgery would enhance our dignity as one made in God's image and likeness.

To consider this question in a larger context we might ask ourselves to look how much is spent on "looking better" when many people have neither food nor shelter nor proper clothing. A good meditation about cosmetic surgery is to think first of Jesus' concern for the poor and then how he wishes to work through us to take care of his poor as the body of Christ.

15. When is it morally acceptable to use anti-depressant medication?

It is morally acceptable to use anti-depressant medications when a medical professional judges them to be the best response to the condition of the patient. Prescribing them presumes the consent of the patient or his guardian. Under these circumstances, it would be morally obligatory for the patient to take the medication. As we learn more about the causes of depression and other disorders that challenge the sense of equilibrium in people, we hope that the most reliable responses may be found and employed to restore a sense of peace to those suffering from these ailments. Indeed, some people have found that the side effects of anti-depressant medication are worse than the disease; hence, we should be careful about concluding that *all* people with depression can be helped by these medications.

Whereas formerly people considered depression to be simply a question of the state of one's mind, affected by events in his or her life, today's understanding is that depression often involves some type of chemical imbalance in the brain, an imbalance that responds quite well to medications. Evaluation and treatment of depression must be done within the context of the person's whole life. For some people the proper response might be some form of counseling or psychotherapy. Another may respond to anti-depressant medication. Still others might find both of these treatments helpful. As each experience of suffering is unique, so, too, must be the response.

Frequently people will be embarrassed to admit to depression or consider it a sign of weakness or an inability to deal with matters in life. Such thinking is of little help in resolving the issue. In light of the variety of causes and helpful responses to depression, it seems safe to say that medications and psychotherapy alone will not be sufficient to manage depression or other disorders of this nature. People who experience depression need the love and support of family and friends to accompany them in the suffering and to assist in their healing.

---

16. Science and medicine have developed gene therapies in response to findings from genetic testing. Are these therapies morally permissible?

We must distinguish between two types of therapies in response to genetic defects: somatic therapy and germ line therapy. Somatic therapy will affect the individual patient who receives the therapy. Germ line therapy will affect not just the one who receives the therapy but also any children born from that person. In the first, the genetic makeup of the patient alone is affected; in the second, the genetic makeup of that person and his or her progeny is altered. In many if not most cases, germ line therapy would take place not on a human being but on a sperm or an egg prior to their being joined in a laboratory to create an embryo.

A second distinction concerns the focus of the therapy. Some therapies attempt to correct a genetic defect as a form of medical treatment. Other therapies might be described as enhancement therapies where one is not attempting to cure a health defect but to make changes not essential to the health of the patient, such as genetic alteration for blue eyes or something of that nature.

The Church has judged that somatic therapy for medical purposes is morally licit as long as there are no disproportionate risks to the patient. In other words, the benefits to be gained from the therapy ought to warrant any risks that the patient might undergo, particularly with this new field of medical therapy. This point would be particularly important if considering somatic therapy on a fetus. Church teaching would oppose therapies carried out for purposes other than medical necessity.

Germ line therapies alter the genetic makeup of an embryo in its earliest stages of life, or the genetic makeup of sperm or egg prior to fertilization. The Church judges that germ line therapies, at least in the present state of research, should be avoided because "the risks connected to any genetic manipulation are considerable and as yet not fully controllable" (*The Dignity of the Person*, #26). A further ethical problem with gene therapy is the creation of embryos outside the natural process of sexual intercourse within marriage.

It must be stated also that genetic research and, more particularly, gene therapies—somatic or germ line—are relatively in the infancy stage of development. While much is known, there is much that remains to be learned so that therapies may indeed be used to further authentic human good.

17. Recently a genetic testing kit became available. Does the Church have any teaching on genetic testing?

In principle the Church is not opposed to genetic testing. Science and medicine's breakthrough in discovering the presence and function of our genes and in detecting, in particular, those genes associated with diseases is an important discovery with long-term consequences for both science and medicine. The number of tests available seems to rise almost daily. The critical issue from a moral standpoint is what we do with the information that is gained.

Any use of the information to harm people in any way would be judged immoral. A specific example of the improper use of genetic information concerns tests that lead to the detection of Down syndrome in a fetus with subsequent abortion of the developing new life. Another example would be using genetic information against people seeking health insurance, employment, and so forth.

Another concern raised about genetic testing is the impact that information might have on the person(s) receiving it. For example, a person may wish to know if he is carrying the gene for Huntington's disease, an illness that will surface in a person's life if he has the gene. There is no cure for this debilitating disease. While it may be helpful for a person to know that he has a genetic predisposition to the disease, the newfound information does not allow him to do anything to treat the disease as such. However, the information may assist him to prepare himself and others for the time when the disease will manifest itself.

In other instances, however, obtaining genetic information may well lead to prevention and treatment of disease. This aspect of genetic testing is the most hopeful and promising. Such testing would also allow spouses to know if they are carriers of a particular gene, for example, that associated with cystic fibrosis. A couple finding themselves carriers of the gene will want to bear this in mind as they make decisions about responsible parenthood.

Summarizing, information obtained from genetic testing holds promise and potential peril. Keeping in mind the equal dignity and life of persons will help to guide judgments about the morally acceptable use of genetic information.

18. A friend of mine had cancer, and all treatments were unsuccessful. She was asked if she wanted to participate in an experimental treatment. She did. Is that OK?

The person's participation in experimental treatment for cancer was most likely morally acceptable. Two key points to bear in mind regarding experimentation on anyone are informed consent and a weighing of the benefits to be gained over the burdens and risks to be endured. This judgment presumes that the person was fully informed about the experimental treatment, its potential for good and harm, and that she judged the benefit to be greater than any burden she would suffer.

Some additional points might be helpful to keep in mind about our participation in experimental therapies. First, therapies should be tested sufficiently on non-humans or even on human cadavers in order to perfect that therapy for use with human beings. Second, just as participation in the experiment presumes that the person understands fully the risks and freely assents to participation, so, too, if the person wishes to stop the experiment, she is free to do so. A final consideration concerns the potential beneficiaries of the experiment. This point may apply in the situation that we just addressed. It is highly possible that the person who undergoes treatment will not be cured and, indeed, may not even be helped (and could be harmed) since these are experimental drugs or interventions. However, her participation in the experiment, while not reaping any successful results for her own cancer, may well contribute to medicine's understanding of cancer therapies and help others. Again, as long as the risks are not disproportionate to the potential benefit, this added motivation for participating in experimental programs is laudable.

Words of caution have to be raised about making judgments for participation in experimental programs for persons other than us. For example, we might be asked to make judgments for our children or for incompetent or unconscious adults, or even our unborn human life. In these cases the clear goal of participation must be the benefit to the person who is ill. Any intervention must be of therapeutic value to the person who is undergoing the experimentation. Although it is possible that information from clinical research will be helpful for others, experimentation on the most vulnerable among us should be done first and foremost only for their benefit.

---

19. Two relatives of mine died from an untreated medical condition because they refused to see a doctor. Is it right to force people to undergo medical treatment when they seem too stubborn or lazy to do something on their own?

The question raises the issue of responsibility for our own life and health and for the life and health of others. It also raises questions of human freedom.

The Catechism refers to physical life and health as "precious gifts entrusted to us by God" (#2288). An important word here is "entrusted" to us. In theological terms we speak of ourselves as stewards, not masters, of our lives and the lives of others. God alone is the author and master of life. We are to use wisely the gifts that have been given to us.

In the present case, the relatives failed in their responsibility to care properly for their own health and life. We do not know why they failed to do so, and we are not in a position to make a judgment about their motives. Fear may have prevented them from seeking assistance. We simply do not know. What we do know is that they did not take proper care of themselves. Understandably their relative wonders what could and should have been done so that things might have turned out differently.

One cannot force someone else to undergo medical treatment. Unless a patient is proved to be incompetent, no medical professional today would treat someone against his will. Apart from seeking legal action to declare someone incompetent and to assume responsibility for that person's medical decisions, one is left with a responsibility to support a relative and to attempt to establish an environment of trust and safety where the person may examine as objectively as possible his present medical condition.

Human experience tells us that one of the most common emotions of those who are suffering in any way is that they feel isolated, detached from others and even from themselves. How frequently do we hear someone who is ill say, "I don't feel myself." Perhaps the best response to people who are unwilling and perhaps afraid to seek medical assistance is to assure them that we will support them in whatever way we are able and to assure them of our prayers for their well-being.

---

20. I recently declared myself an organ donor. What does the Church teach about organ donation? Is there any difference in teaching for someone who is alive or for someone who has died?

Several years ago, before he became Pope Benedict XVI, Cardinal Joseph Ratzinger called organ donation an "act of love." Pope John Paul II wrote in *The Gospel of Life* that organ donation is a gesture of self-giving love when "performed in an ethically acceptable manner, with a view to offering a chance of health and even of life itself to the sick who sometimes have no other hope"(#86). News reports inform us constantly that the demand for organ donors far outweighs the response. The Church's support for this practice is significant and consistent with its value of human life.

What conditions surrounding organ donation would comprise what the pope called "an ethically acceptable manner?" The main issue for both live and cadaver donation is the free and informed consent of the person. In cases of live organ donation, for example, kidney, liver, bone marrow, or stem cells, the donor must be aware of risks involved in the procedure and is obliged ethically not to put herself in unreasonable danger while pursuing the praiseworthy goal of helping someone else. There should also be no economic benefit attached to donating organs (See USCCB *Ethical and Religious Directives for Health Care Services*, #30).

When organ donation involves those who have died, the critical moral issue is that the donor has died prior to the process of harvesting organs for donation to others. Because of advances in technology, it is possible to keep body organs functioning after a person is declared dead. Preventing the deterioration of organs is most important for successful transplants. A danger, however, is that the demand for organs might move people to begin the process before the donor has died. Doing so would not only be an affront to the dignity of the dying person but also would place extra burdens on his or her family. One must be absolutely certain that death has occurred according to standard medical criteria before allowing for organ donation. This final point is all the more in order if and when someone might make a judgment for another about organ donation, as for example, in the death of an infant or child.

21. May I donate my body to science? And what happens after?

Catholics may donate their bodies to science or for medical education in the training of medical students. The reasoning is similar to that regarding organ donation. It is viewed as an act of charity toward those who may benefit in any way from the study of a particular disease that took the life of the deceased or from other research that may be done using the body of one who has died. The recently revised *Ethical and Religious Directives for Catholic Health Care Services* states: "Catholic healthcare institutions should encourage and provide the means whereby those who wish to do so may arrange for the donation of their organs and bodily tissue, for ethically legitimate purposes, so that they may be used for donation and research after death." (ERD #63).

As in the case of organ donation, the critical issue with donating one's body to science is informed consent. That is, a person has been fully apprised of what will happen to his body upon its donation and acceptance.

Because the Catholic tradition has such respect for the human body, we would want to be sure that the body is properly respected when scientific study is finished. Ordinarily this would entail cremation of the body. As a general rule, several bodies that have been used in study would be cremated at the same time. Family members may request that the cremated remains be given back to them for burial in a family plot. They must understand, however, that when several bodies are cremated at once, the ashes received will be part of the remains from all those who were cremated at once. It is also helpful to know that frequently there will be a considerable gap from the time when a body is donated to science and the cremated remains are returned to the family, if that was the request of the family.

22. I feel guilty about putting my mother in a nursing home. Have I abandoned her?

Although many people today might encourage us to live guilt-free lives, guilt is actually a morally healthy response in many situations. Genuine guilt should arise when we do not do what we ought to do or when we have done something that is clearly wrong. If we cannot swim and do not jump in the water to save a person who is drowning, we should not feel guilty. We did not possess the skills to save the person. If we fail to call for help, however, we have done wrong and should experience healthy guilt. Again, the key to authentic guilt is assessing one's ability to respond to the situation at hand in the best way possible.

Caring for one's aging and fragile parents is a responsibility that is increasing as people live longer and are assisted in doing so by advances in medical technology. Accompanying longer lives, however, is often poorer health. Frequently family members judge that they do not believe that they have the wherewithal to care responsibly for their parents. As a result, they seek a nursing facility where their parents may be properly cared for in terms of their health in its physical, psychological, and even spiritual aspects. For example, nursing homes with a trained staff that understand the needs of the elderly may be of great assistance to our loved one. They have experience with many elderly residents, while our experience may be limited to our own loved one.

The issue can be more complicated in cases where parents (and others) will ask their children to promise "never to put me into a nursing home." As difficult as it is to refuse this request, neither you nor your parent knows how much care will be needed, and a promise is not fair to the family. The best response would be to say, "We will look after you as long as we possibly can, and we would only consider a nursing home if your care needs were greater than what we could handle or if it were the only place where you could be safely cared for."

Nothing substitutes for our own ongoing care and attention to our parents and loved ones. Sometimes guilt arises in situations raised in this question because we have not had the best relationship with a parent and perhaps regret and feel guilt about things from our past. The best way to respond in moments like these is to learn from the past and move forward. If our relationship was marked by a lack of attention to our parents, we might commit to being more attentive now, even though they do not live with us. We would fail in our love for our parents only by entrusting them to the care of others and then depriving them of our love and affection. That would be the worst form of abandonment.

---

23. Two relatives of mine died from a disease for which they never sought treatment. Both were people of faith and said: "God will heal me if that is his will." Wouldn't God have wanted them to see a doctor?

It is safe to say that God would have them see a doctor. Does doing so compromise our faith in God? People might point to a text from sacred Scripture like Jesus' words from the Sermon on the Mount where he encourages people not to be concerned about their lives, food, clothing, and so forth (Matthew 6). He even asks: "And can any of you by worrying add a single hour to your span of life?" He concludes this section by saying that our heavenly Father knows our needs and will take care of us. Our task is to focus on God's kingdom.

Despite texts like these, throughout all of salvation history God has relied on human beings to be his instruments, his messengers. This point is shown most fully in Jesus becoming human for our salvation. So, while we believe in a God who can and has acted miraculously throughout history, these moments are exceptions, not the rule. Ordinarily God's work is done by human hands. The spread of the Gospel itself has come about through people who have responded to God in faith.

Part of this Gospel story is the healing ministry of Jesus. Christianity has from the beginning taken up Jesus' ministry of healing and attempted to restore health to the sick not only through prayer and the sacraments but also through institutions to care for the sick and the dying. From the earliest times, however, Christianity has also put the care of our physical bodies in a subordinate role to our relationship with God. If care for our bodies and a preoccupation with material things were to get in the way of our spiritual lives, then we would rightly be concerned.

Recognizing the primary goal of our relationship with God, we must also see that caring for our lives and our health, gifts from that same God, is a responsible way to receive and be good stewards of these gifts. Trusting in God we seek out those means of medicine to care properly for our physical bodies. Properly attending to our physical health and seeking professional medical assistance when necessary enables us to live fully in relationship with God.

One further thought: Think of the training/knowledge/experience that doctors and nurses and all other healthcare practitioners have spent years attaining. Is not their work a miracle of God's love when it brings healing, restoration, and renewal? Why might we not see their work as God's ways of healing or God's ways of performing miracles?

24. Must I visit the sick, even when they are unconscious or if they are awake but do not recognize me?

From the earliest days of the Christian community, visiting the sick has been a part of discipleship in Christ. We are given a clear example in Jesus' ministry of care for the sick and are instructed by Jesus to be particularly attentive to visiting the sick because in doing so, we visit him (Matthew 25). The ministries of celebrating the sacrament of anointing of the sick, hospital chaplaincy, extraordinary ministers of Communion from parish communities, and the kindness of individuals continue this work of Jesus in our own day.

Perhaps the heart of this question, however, is whether sick persons know that we are visiting. Are they unconscious and unaware of our presence? Are we visiting a parent or a loved one who no longer seems to recognize us? We might ask what the benefit is of visiting in this case.

Two points might be made about this scenario. The first concerns the person we visit, the second concerns us.

Although a person we visit may not know us, we know him. His human contact with us is important in whatever way that occurs. We recall a woman saying that she simply held and massaged the hands of a woman with Alzheimer's disease just so she would know that someone was there.

Despite diagnoses of lack of consciousness and our experience of people with dementia or Alzheimer's disease, some "unconscious" patients have later reported being able to hear what was going on around them. Similarly, there are reported incidents of people with Alzheimer's disease who suddenly and inexplicably have moments of lucidity. These situations would clearly be the exception if they were to ever occur. But they point to the inherent limits of our understanding of diseases and their effect on the minds of those who suffer from them.

The second point about visiting the sick concerns us. Quite simply, visiting the sick is a way of living our dignity as people made in the image and likeness of God. Peter Maurin of the Catholic Worker movement once described people in need as ambassadors of God. As such, he said, they deserve the attention and care of those who could give it. The sick may be considered ambassadors of God. Their presence gives us an opportunity to become Godlike, to come out of ourselves in selfless love and care for another. Visiting them not only connects us to them and to God whose ambassadors they are, it also helps us to live more fully the dignity that we possess as children of God.

Chapter 3

INTRODUCTION TO
END OF LIFE SECTION

When patients learn that their life is soon to end, both the persons concerned and their loved ones can display a wide range of responses. Some people of faith, while not denying that death is inevitable, will try to postpone it as long as possible; others might not wish any life-prolonging measures and face death with faith and hope, eventually leading to acceptance.

Dying and death can produce fear, anxiety, anger, awe, a sense of hopelessness, courage, hope, and faith. While Christians believe that death is the end of life on earth and the beginning of another life in eternity, they still have to navigate the journey of dying in their unique and personal way. For some, the overriding feeling may be one of dependency, due to their severe incapacities, of suffering and a sense of isolation because they cannot do the things they once enjoyed, or of disappointment, due to a lack of support from family and friends. For others, the main focus may be a sense of urgency so as to make the most of the days, weeks, or months that remain. We may well see people experiencing all of these feelings at one time or another. One's faith in all these contexts may grow and be a source of great comfort, or it may be marked by doubt and crisis.

Our Catholic tradition not only reaffirms that God created each of us for eternal life, that our God is compassionate and God's grace will sustain us, it also calls us to be servants to others and channels of God's grace, especially for those in need and those most vulnerable. In other words, how we die, how we experience our dying, greatly depends on the trust and confidence we can place in the compassion and care of our God, family, friends, faith community, the physician, and healthcare workers.

In Catholic spiritual writings, suffering and death are often referred to as mysteries. They are indeed mysterious because we never understand them fully or really answer the many questions linked to these profound experiences. For example, why does God allow some people to live long lives and others short lives? Why is it that some have sudden deaths and others a long drawn-out dying process? Why does God allow some to suffer for long periods of time while others have a brief and peaceful dying process and death? What really happens to us and our loved ones when we die, and what is heaven like? Ultimately each person has a quest to find a meaning to his life and his death, and we all deserve to experience the final phases of our journey with a sense of dignity and spiritual support. We believe that the following questions and our responses can be informative for those asking practical questions on the experience of dying on the part of the patient, the physician, the family and one's friends. However such questions and responses will not reveal the full mystery of death and dying nor address all the practical and spiritual dimensions of this experience of being human.

While not denying the anxiety and suffering that can accompany the last cycle of life for Christians nor the moral complexity of many contemporary medical options now open to us, we believe that, for persons of faith, their experience will be grounded and transformed in the Christ who suffered and died that we might have eternal life. Illness and the dying process can often provide us with an opportunity to reaffirm or rediscover our faith in Christ, humanity, and the resurrection.

25. Must we always preserve life?

One of the most agonizing experiences that we can have is to make a decision about whether to continue medical treatment for ourselves or for a family member. Many of us attempt to deal with this question by expressing our wishes in writing just in case we would not be able to speak for ourselves. However, no preparation ever equips us fully for weighty decisions about preserving human life.

The short answer to the question, "Must we always preserve life?" is "no."

However, because we live in cultural environments that often do not respect the dignity of all human life, no matter how healthy or sick a person may be, we must be clear as to why we are not always obliged to preserve human life.

The Church offers clear moral guidance in this area, always calling us to show respect for persons and concern for their welfare. The fundamental teaching is that human life is the most basic gift that we receive, but it is a gift given for higher goals, not as an end itself. For example, we adore Jesus Christ, who offered his life out of love for us. We venerate martyrs who sacrificed their lives in order to witness to Christ. In secular society we honor heroes who offer their lives to save and protect others. Our physical bodies and the gift of life are necessary for us to be alive and have a relationship with God and others. But we recognize human life as a temporary good, something that will pass, as we all must die.

We ought to live and respect human life in a middle ground between clinging to life at all costs, what is called vitalism, and disregarding human life and disrespecting persons in the process. This middle ground recognizes the gift of life and encourages us to be good stewards of life but acknowledges that we are not the masters of our own lives. God alone is the giver of life.

Sometimes the most responsible decision judges further medical treatment and aggressive care as too much for us and for others. Church teaching calls these medical measures extraordinary or disproportionate. In other words, preserving life at these times would work against the higher goods for which we were created. An ongoing question that we might ask ourselves is how we are to live and preserve our lives so that we give and receive love to and from God and others. Sometimes that will urge us to preserve life; other times it will move us to let go.

26. How can you know whether a measure to preserve life is ordinary or extraordinary?

This distinction in the Catholic moral tradition dating back at least to the Dominican theologian Francisco de Vitoria in the sixteenth century, was included in the moral writings of Saint Alphonsus Liguori in the eighteenth century and has been emphasized and developed in the teachings of recent popes. The distinction revolves around benefits and burdens to the patient and also the benefits and burdens to others.

Basically, if a medical procedure is judged to be ordinary, there is a moral obligation to use it, and if it is judged to be extraordinary, then its use is optional. Sometimes Church documents and theologians refer to proportionate and disproportionate rather than ordinary and extraordinary means so that the entire person's life is considered, rather than focusing solely on the medical procedure. This latter practice still happens with some frequency.

It is very important to understand that ordinary and extraordinary do not refer to treatments themselves but only to those offered to a particular patient in his unique context. For example, you cannot answer the question: "Is a ventilator ordinary or extraordinary treatment?" without considering the uniqueness of each patient's physical and moral resources.

How do we separate ordinary from extraordinary in practice? Church teaching gives us some guidelines. We are instructed to consider the following: the type of treatment to be used, its degree of complexity or risk, the cost of the treatment, the possibilities of actually using it, the burdens it will place on the patient and others, and the positive results that can be expected. All of these factors are to be weighed and considered in a particular context, namely, taking into account the state of the person, that is, considering the treatment in the light of the patient's physical, spiritual, and moral resources (Sacred Congregation for the Doctrine of the Faith, *Declaration on Euthanasia*, section 4).

Thus determining the ordinary or extraordinary means of preserving life is not just the weighing of burdens and benefits, of effectiveness and cost, but also the consideration of the physical, moral, and spiritual resources of a particular person who will experience the burdens and benefits.

In other words, the use of a respirator, dialysis, or standard treatments for pneumonia may be judged ordinary means for one patient but extraordinary for another because of differing medical, moral, and spiritual circumstances. Further, we should not confuse ordinary and extraordinary means with non-experimental and experimental because a non-experimental procedure such as angioplasty (the surgical reconstruction of blood vessels) may or may not be an extraordinary means to prolong someone's life, depending on his overall condition determined by the many factors we addressed earlier.

27. What is the difference between medical intervention and basic healthcare?

Medical interventions to restore health, alleviate pain, or prolong life usually require medical professionals. Other activities such as ensuring cleanliness and warmth, feeding, the giving of giving water, and respecting the personal dignity belong to basic healthcare, sometimes referred to as natural care. Church statements give the impression that all forms of natural care are normally obligatory. Of course there can come a time when it is unreasonable to force a dying patient to eat or drink in the normal fashion because such an insistence is too burdensome for the patient and there is very little to be gained.

Perhaps we should include spiritual care of the person under the heading of natural care. Here, too, we need to be sensitive to the condition of the patient. Sometimes a faith-filled dying person may ask family members to tone down vocal prayers, as wonderful as they may be, because noise causes her pain or agitation. There are appropriate and inappropriate times to raise spiritual matters with the sick and dying.

One may ask if artificial nutrition and hydration are a medical intervention or natural basic healthcare? Interestingly John Paul II in 2004 stated: "I should like, particularly, to underline how the administration of water and food, even when provided by artificial means, always represents a natural means of preserving life, not a medical act" (John Paul II, "To the participants in the International Congress on 'Life-Sustaining Treatments and Vegetative State: Scientific Advances and Ethical Dilemmas,'" #4). The pope goes on to state that, in principle, such nutrition and hydration are morally obligatory until they have attained their proper finality, which is providing nourishment and alleviating suffering. So, in the case where a patient's body can no longer process such nutrition or hydration or its administration causes them more suffering, we would have a situation where what is normally natural care is causing more burden than benefit and would cease to be obligatory. The fact that an action is termed natural care does not necessarily imply that it cannot be judged extraordinary in certain circumstances. In fact, it is well-known that both Pope John Paul II and Cardinal John O'Connor refused nutrition and hydration when it had become an extraordinary measure for the preservation of life, when it had become an excessive burden, or when their bodies could no longer assimilate the nutrients provided.

28. What is a living will?

A competent person may draw up a document or complete a form which gives instructions regarding the type of treatment he desires if he finds himself in a situation where he can no longer communicate his wishes regarding his medical treatment. Such a document is referred to as a living will.

Usually what appears in a living will is the directive to be allowed to die and not to be kept alive by extraordinary means, especially if there is little hope of recovery from severe physical or mental disability. Of course a person could leave a very different type of directive indicating that he wants all means employed to preserve his life. A living will, if it does not rule out ordinary or proportionate means of preserving life, is not in conflict with the Catholic moral tradition. Such a will could simply be making it clear to the physician and the family that a person does not want extraordinary means used to preserve his life if there is no hope of recovery from extreme physical and mental disability.

However, given the fact that most people do not complete a living will, it can be very useful and comforting for the family and the physician if a person has at least spoken about such matters and given some indication in conversation as to what he would want if he found himself in a situation where he was unable to communicate or make a competent decision. In fact, such communication or indication is important even if a person has an advance directive, such as a living will or durable power of attorney, for how can a document foresee every medical eventuality that could arise? In other words, it can be very difficult to interpret the document and apply the directives in concrete and unforeseen circumstances.

As we have observed, it is difficult to determine whether a means to prolong life is ordinary or extraordinary, proportionate or disproportionate. A statement in a living will to the effect that one does not wish to have extraordinary means used to preserve his life of course begs the question of what is extraordinary for him in his present physical and spiritual state given his diagnosis and prognosis. Only detailed directives in a living will and the communication to family of one's attitude to life, death, health, and faith will help others make the right decision based on one's wishes if such a situation should arise.

Many people who write advance directives also appoint a substitute decision maker (or proxy, or in some states, a power of attorney for healthcare matters) who can make decisions for the no-longer-competent person. One can make the proxy the final chooser, limit the proxy with written instructions, or provide written instructions for the proxy rather than the healthcare team. See the questions following to understand how a proxy can be combined with written instructions, especially in complex situations where nobody could anticipate the issues or decisions that need to be made.

29. Who makes decisions about treatment or refusal of treatment?

The moral obligation to use ordinary or proportionate means to preserve life falls normally to the patient. Even if the patient refuses such treatment, as long as she is competent, such a refusal is generally acknowledged by law. The fact that the state or the law may accept a competent patient's refusal of ordinary means of preserving life does not mean the decision is objectively right. We can think of the example of the patient refusing a blood transfusion for religious reasons, which could be an ordinary means of preserving life. The Church maintains that we have a moral obligation to accept ordinary means to preserve our life. Determining what is ordinary for a particular person in a particular circumstance is the crucial task.

A patient, because of the complexity of the proposed medical options, and because he has confidence in a family member or friend to understand the medical information better than he can, may ask another person to make the decisions for him. Asking another to act in such a way on his part is not a declaration that he sees himself as incompetent. Rather it is the exercise of his rational opinion that another can make the best decisions for him in a particular medical situation. We call this other person a "proxy" with durable power of attorney.

There may be cases where family or culture actually usurps the decision-making process from a competent person and the patient only gives the impression that it is her own free decision. Physicians and family need to be aware that sometimes patients in these stressful times of their lives feel coerced by strong family views but do not give voice to this experience of being manipulated.

Underlying this question is the actual meaning of "competence." Ordinarily we consider someone competent when she is able to give free and informed consent to a particular medical procedure or to refuse treatment freely and knowingly. What constitutes sufficient freedom and knowledge for a competent decision has plagued moral theologians for centuries. To be competent does not mean that we make a stand-alone decision on our own disregarding or not listening to the advice of experts, family, and the Church. Rather it means that a patient, with the help of others, actually can understand the diagnosis and prognosis, can weigh the benefits and burdens of accepting proposed treatments or rejecting them, and can make a decision freely.

For the person of faith, not only does the information given to him need to be in a form free from medical jargon so that he can really understand the options and the consequences of the various options, the same information needs to be taken to prayer so that wisdom and understanding, the gifts of the Holy Spirit, will influence the decisions.

30. Who makes decisions when a patient is no longer competent?

When a patient is no longer competent to make a decision about his treatment, a surrogate may make the decisions for him. We say that the surrogate has been given durable power of attorney for healthcare matters. That is a legal instrument that specifies a surrogate or proxy to make medical decisions on behalf of the patient if he becomes incompetent. Such a surrogate or proxy has to work within certain limits. Knowing what the patient would have wanted in the medical circumstances at hand, because of previous conversations on such topics, the surrogate cannot simply ignore such wishes of the patient and make her own decisions bypassing these wishes.

If the person with the durable power of attorney for healthcare matters lacks expressed directives from the patient (for example, a living will), he cannot choose to withdraw or withhold treatment when it is judged that such treatment is in the best interests of the patient. In most cases what a particular patient would want in a concrete situation is not explicitly stated or clear and so the criterion of the best interests of the patient is employed. To gauge the best interests of the patient, the weighing of benefits and burdens to the patient has to be carried out. From a Catholic perspective, it is always in the person's best interests to provide ordinary means of preserving life, keeping in mind that the judgment of ordinary and proportionate is made in light of the broad understanding of health for the patient.

When it comes to the person with the durable power of attorney for healthcare matters withdrawing or withholding extraordinary means of preserving life, how much evidence of the patient's wishes is required? A living will may make the surrogate's task easier but, failing this, what is a surrogate to do? Famous cases, such as the Nancy Cruzan case in Missouri in 1990, have highlighted conflicting views in the law and in the interpretation of Catholic moral teaching. Nancy Cruzan was a 30-year-old woman who was diagnosed as suffering from a persistent vegetative state after a car accident. Her wishes about treatment in these circumstances were not known, or at least not clear. Her parents fought a long legal battle to allow the doctors to remove her feeding tube, which brought about her death from the effects of dehydration and malnutrition.

A state or country may require, before a surrogate could make a choice about forgoing certain treatment, that there be clear and convincing evidence that a patient, when he was competent, did not wish to have these procedures employed if he were in a certain medical condition. While the law is the law in a particular state or country, failing the existence of such a law, the Catholic tradition could argue that the withdrawal of extraordinary means of preserving life could be in the patient's best interest in his particular circumstances, even without clear and convincing evidence that this is what he actually wanted.

31. What is the practical difference between two types of advance directives such as a living will and assigning a healthcare proxy?

Both a living will and the designation of a healthcare proxy (sometimes called a "durable power of attorney for healthcare matters") are documents that take effect if a patient becomes incompetent. The first document specifies the medical procedures the patient wishes to receive and also to avoid. The second type of document specifies a particular person to make medical decision on a patient's behalf should that person become incompetent. A healthcare proxy is sometimes referred to simply as a "proxy" or "surrogate."

The limitation of the living will is that no directive can look into the future and predict all medical conditions or circumstances that may arise. Usually, therefore, such a directive may need to focus on general principles or goals rather than itemizing particular medical procedures. The benefit of assigning a healthcare proxy with the durable power of attorney for healthcare matters is that the proxy can, drawing on her personal knowledge of the patient, use discretion to make decisions in changing and sometimes unexpected circumstances. Obviously one should choose a person who not only knows the teachings of the Church and one's own preferences but who is also capable of making decisions under pressure and applying general principles to very concrete situations.

You can also write an advance directive specifically for your proxy who then, in conversation with your medical care team, makes all the decisions for you, based upon your known wishes and his/her best understanding of you. The advantage of this lies in not having the doctors interpret your written instructions without really knowing you.

32. May you have recourse to pain relief even though it hastens death?

One may take positive steps to lessen a dying person's pain even though a drug used may hasten his death. In such a difficult situation it is essential that one does not directly intend the death of the patient but rather directly intends the relief of pain. The Catholic tradition has drawn upon the principle of double effect to help us deal with such a case. The principle states that:

The act itself is not an act of killing. In this case the act itself is one of administering a drug to relieve pain.

The bad effect is not caused by the good effect. In this case the bad effect, hastening one's death, is not caused by the good effect, the relief of pain. Rather, the act of administering a drug causes two effects equally: the good effect and the bad effect. In other words we truly have a double effect.

The intention of the moral agent must be good. In this case the intention of the person administering the drug or asking that it be administered is not to cause directly the death of the patient, rather the direct intention is to relieve pain.

Finally, the bad effect needs to be in proportion to the good effect. In this case the good effect of relieving pain would be judged to outweigh the indirect bad effect of shortening life.

In the Catholic tradition, the roots of the principle of double effect go back centuries. Its application to pain relief has been employed more recently by popes Pius XII and John Paul II. On a practical level, the real intention of the nurse administering the drug, or the patient or family of the patient asking for the pain-relieving drug, can be clarified often by a simple question: "Would you prefer that the patient's life not be shortened if there were some other way to relieve their pain?"

With the advances today in palliative/hospice care at the end of life, morphine and other pain control medications are used with great care. It is seldom the case that morphine will shorten one's life by lowering the breathing rate of a patient.

Hence, the principle of double effect will be used most often in an intensive-care unit, where a patient may be suffering great pain but has many other medical problems that make the use of morphine more delicate. Nonetheless, the principle of double effect allows the physician to concentrate on controlling pain as a priority for the dying.

When the patient finally dies one may feel a sense of relief for him and for oneself and one's family. Such a feeling of relief does not necessarily imply that one wanted to hasten the patient's death through pain relief, be that relief given through drugs or other medical procedures. Rather, death is seen and felt as a blessing because the person is now at rest, and we were able to lessen his pain during the dying process.

33. May a person refuse pain relief, and, if so, why?

It may seem odd at first glance that a person would prefer to endure pain. Some patients choose this route because they mistakenly believe that pain medications will shorten their life (studies have shown this not to be true). Others realize that pain medications will often make a person drowsy or downright sleepy, but they want to stay as alert as possible to live their lives and to be as attentive as possible to family and loved ones.

Palliative care is well aware of the importance of living for the dying. These caregivers understand that a patient may need time to put her affairs in good order, to attend to family matters, to prepare for death, to be reconciled with her God and others, or to say the necessary goodbyes. Palliative care staff always works with the patient (or the non-competent patient's family) to balance all the factors necessary to allow the patient to be as alert as possible and to be as pain-free as possible.

Some people also believe that the acceptance of pain is part of their spiritual life or religious duty. For example, some Christians would see themselves as sharing in the sufferings of Christ, who has loved them and blessed them in life and will care for them in death. Such a person could make the decision that it is better to endure pain so as to be able to consciously interact with others.

Accepting pain for any reason is the patient's choice. However, three things need to be pointed out. First, God does not expect people to suffer. That is why there are capable doctors and good medications (and other treatments) for pain control. Second, pain can get out of control and then it is impossible to concentrate on prayer, visiting family, or doing anything other than stoically gritting one's teeth. It would dishonor Christ to think that he asks anybody to put up with such pain. To paraphrase his words, there are enough troubles in life without having to choose what is avoidable. And, third, when a patient's pain begins to disturb others—nearby patients hearing moans and even screams, or family members who are agitated by seeing their loved one in pain, or medical caregivers who are unable to care properly for a patient because of the level of untreated pain—then a patient has no right to refuse pain control medication for any pious or personal reason.

While answering this question and the previous one we have been using the narrower term "pain" rather than the broader term "suffering." The dying can suffer from more than physical pain, and these sufferings need more than medical procedures and drugs. There may be the fear of death, a sense of loneliness or isolation, a feeling of being a burden on one's family and friends, or not wanting to leave this world because of the suffering it will cause to others. Such suffering can really only be relieved by human understanding, human interaction, compassion, reassurance, faith, prayer, and a willingness to let a person leave this world and return to her Creator.

There is another reason why a dying person or his family may refuse certain drugs to relieve pain, namely the fear of addiction. While addiction can be a real issue for the person on the road to recovery or with a reasonable life expectancy, it should be obvious that ongoing addiction is not a moral issue for the dying patient whose time is short and whose physician is aware of his needs regarding consciousness and pain relief.

34. What does palliative/hospice care mean?

Palliative care specializes in caring for sick and dying persons in all their needs. An obvious need may be the managing of physical pain and discomfort by advanced knowledge of palliative medicine. But full palliative care would also consider the spiritual, emotional and social needs of the sick and dying person as well. Hospices for the dying acknowledge there is no cure for the dying person, so they concentrate on holistic care and concern.

Patients may wish to speak to a chaplain or ordained member of the clergy to be able to make sense of their condition or even prepare themselves for their approaching death, so those working in palliative care would need to be sensitive to this spiritual need. The physical environment of the hospital or hospice can make a considerable difference for both the patient and his loved ones. In fact, the trend in many places today is to use hospice care like home care where patients are in familiar surroundings. At institutional hospices, however, a room with large windows enables one to see the sun, sky, or garden and so remain aware of the beginning and the ending of days. A gathering place, where relatives and friends can meet, take a break or simply be alone to gather thoughts and strength can make the journey of accompanying a sick or dying person less stressful.

The attitude and patience of the nursing staff contribute greatly to the emotional well-being of the patient and the family. The way sick and dying persons are spoken to and the manner in which their bodies are handled can either respect or disrespect the patient's dignity. Catholic hospitals and hospices, in particular, should be specialists in palliative care, for they are caring for the sons and daughters of God at a most vulnerable time of their lives.

35. Should we always tell persons that they are dying?

In the past, and to a certain extent in some cultures today, there was and still can be a paternalistic attitude of doctors toward their patients. This attitude could be expressed by a doctor deciding not to tell patients the real state of their health lest the anxiety caused by such truth telling could slow their recovery. A patient could not even be informed that he is actually dying because, in the judgment of the doctor and/or the family, such distressing information would lead the person to a sense of hopelessness and despair or hasten death.

Today, patients' rights to know the truth about their condition and their prognosis is given far greater emphasis, even if they are dying. After all, people have a right to know their diagnosis and prognosis for the many reasons mentioned in the previous question about pain relief and the shortening of life. For example, one may need to attend to personal, financial, spiritual, and familial matters before death. Furthermore, without such information, how could a patient make an informed decision about the type of treatment he should have or forgo? In short, denying a person the truth is misplaced compassion.

Difficult situations do arise, and this is when the manner of telling the truth to the patient can make a difference. The words used, the amount of information given at a particular time, the availability of the doctor or other healthcare workers to answer questions, and the support of the family when the news is given can make the difference between truth telling that respects the rights of the patient to know and truth telling that simply leaves a person in despair and confusion. Many experts on death and dying claim that people often have a sense that they are in the dying process even when others may not wish to talk about this reality with them. Secrecy becomes a barrier that inhibits real communication about the most important aspects of life and death.

Dedicated people trained in pastoral care have an important role when it comes to the effects of hearing the truth. Their compassion and counseling skills can help family and friends realize that the issue is not so much the decision to tell or not to tell but rather how to tell a person that he is dying and how best to support him in the dying process.

Occasionally a patient does not want to know his diagnosis or prognosis, much less make decisions about the possible treatments available. Doctors are usually upset by this because their job is to inform the patients fully so they can make the best choices for themselves. Nonetheless, it is very easy for doctors and for families to deal with this situation. The doctor simply asks the patient if she wants to know the diagnosis, what the possible scenarios into the future might be, and what the treatment options are. If the patient does not want to know and, for example, says, "Tell my spouse," then the doctor has fulfilled his job (informing the patient) and can now deal with the spouse as the authorized substitute decision maker.

36. What is euthanasia, and why is it wrong?

The direct killing of an innocent person is always wrong. While the word "euthanasia" literally means a "good or happy death" in Greek and is commonly referred to as "mercy killing," in the Catholic tradition it refers to the direct killing of the innocent person in order that all suffering may be eliminated. One is not permitted to ask for this kind of killing either for herself or for another person entrusted to her care. The Church refers to euthanasia as a violation of the divine law, an offense against the dignity of the human person, and a crime against life.

We need to make some important distinctions about euthanasia. First, it may be voluntary, that is the person asks for her life to be terminated. On the other hand, it may be involuntary, that is, the patient may not ask for her life to be terminated but another individual or authority makes such a decision. Saying that one could not bear to see a person suffer does not detract from the fact that involuntary euthanasia is objectively an act of murder.

Second, euthanasia may be performed in an active manner, for example, the giving of a life-terminating drug, or by the withholding of ordinary means of preserving life. In the past, some people have used the phrase "passive euthanasia," but this is a poor choice of words. Euthanasia presupposes the intention to end the life of the patient. Withholding or removing treatment may in fact simply allow the patient to die (from the underlying disease) and is not necessarily done in order to kill the patient. Thus, it would be better to avoid the phrase "passive euthanasia," with the inherent confusion it carries.

It is important to repeat that when a treatment is withheld or withdrawn because it imposes an excessive burden and is no longer beneficial to the patient, we have a case of forgoing or withdrawing extraordinary means, not euthanasia. One is simply allowing the natural course of a person's life to continue to its natural conclusion by not providing an excessively burdensome or futile treatment. Some states and countries have legalized voluntary euthanasia but evidence shows that such legislation can lead to illegal euthanasia, that is, euthanasia without the consent of the patient. It is important to state that legalizing euthanasia does not make it ethical.

A person may request euthanasia by reason of prolonged pain and discomfort or a feeling that her life is no longer worth living. It is worth considering if a person asking for death is in fact asking for help, for better pain management, and ultimately for a sense of being wanted and loved. As with suicide, the Church acknowledges that the guilt of individuals who request euthanasia may be reduced or completely absent because of their state of mind and circumstances, but it firmly maintains that it is still a direct act of killing the innocent and is morally wrong.

37. Why do some patients desire physician-assisted suicide (PAS)?

A variety of reasons may move a patient to request a lethal dose of medication from his physician to self-administer when he feels ready. Initially, it may be a means of pushing the physician to be honest about his prognosis and to affirm that his suffering will be managed effectively throughout the dying process. However, surveys and studies of patients inquiring about PAS suggest that fear of physical suffering is not the main reason but rather the fear of loss of control, the inability to do the things in life that are enjoyable, the loss of dignity, the feeling of being a burden to family and healthcare personnel.

For many, the consideration and inquiry can act as a kind of backup security just in case these concerns become unbearable for them. Again, studies often reveal that as death draws closer some who considered PAS at the beginning of their terminal diagnosis no longer seriously contemplate such action. If such a request or consideration is made known to a physician or family member, it should be explored rather than dismissed out of hand because the patient is attempting to communicate how he is feeling, what he fears, and even what he is imagining. A sense of worth rather than meaninglessness in the dying process needs to be fostered through compassion, connection with loved ones, and expert spiritual and medical care. And there may be some needs revealed—like pain issues or spiritual suffering—that a good healthcare team (or some member thereof) can help to alleviate or cope with better.

38. Is suicide the same as euthanasia?

Euthanasia is a broader term than suicide. Euthanasia can be performed with or without the consent of the person put to death. Suicide, on the other hand, refers to the killing of oneself. Patients may directly take their own life or, if they find it difficult to terminate their life, ask the assistance of a physician, which is often called physician-assisted suicide. The Catholic

Church condemns suicide because it is contrary to the love that we ought to have for ourselves; it breaks bonds with and is a failure in responsibility to family, neighbors, and brothers and sisters throughout the world; and it is a failure in love of God, who gave us the gift of life (see the Catechism, 2281).

Many people raise a past practice of the Church, namely, refusing to bury people who had committed suicide in consecrated ground. This practice presumed that there was subjective guilt and that the choice to terminate one's life was the result of a free and rational decision. Such a presumption is not made today. The reasons for suicide can be complex and often never fully understood. With advanced knowledge in medicine and psychology (for example, greater insights into clinical depression), one would be slow to conclude that a person was completely free and rational when he took his own life.

Physician-assisted suicide is a form of voluntary euthanasia and involves the physician in an active and formal cooperation in an objectively wrong action. The term "formal" cooperation is used to indicate that the physician, even though he may not administer the actual drug, helps in other ways (prescribing the drug), wills the death of the person, and has an essential role in causing his death. Special attention needs to be given to the prevention of suicide particularly among the most vulnerable groups in our society rather than just condemning the act of suicide.

People who have lost family members and friends to suicide need the care and support of the community and the Church. Family and friends can blame themselves for a suicide, thinking that they should have done more or been more aware of a person's distress. Such self blame is nearly always unfounded, and other friends and family members can hopefully bring the person concerned to realize this. A person who has lost a loved one to suicide may have to deal with her own anger and need support to deal with the nagging question: "How could he or she do this to us, knowing all the pain and distress it would cause us?"

39. Is withholding or withdrawing life support a form of euthanasia?

While it is always morally wrong to directly kill an innocent person, it can sometimes be morally right to allow a person to die. This point implies that it is sometimes morally wrong to allow a person to die. To withhold antibiotics from a person who has every chance of full recovery and living a full life if given the medication would be morally wrong.

But there may be a time in our lives when we have to face the fact that our death is inevitable and that additional medical treatment will place an excessive burden on us and our caretakers, with little benefit. To refuse such treatment is not a form of suicide; rather it is a decision to allow the dying process to take its natural course. The key words here are "excessive burden" and "little benefit." When is the use of the medical treatment of a respirator too burdensome to bear and able to be withdrawn? When is the natural care of nutrition and hydration failing to do what it ought to do? Such life-sustaining treatment or natural care may be too burdensome for some but not for others. One would need to ask the questions we posed in our discussion of ordinary and extraordinary means, medical intervention, and basic healthcare.

A person may not be dying but still wish to refuse certain medical treatments or forms of care because the burden is deemed too great for him and the benefits too little. A young person after a car accident may be left a quadriplegic and is only able to breathe with the help of a respirator, but the thought of living this way for the rest of his life might still be too much for him to bear. He might, in this case, consider the respirator sustaining his life to constitute an extraordinary means of preserving his life and discontinue its use. Such a judgment, however, should not be made without careful consideration, medical and spiritual consultation, and a well-formed conscience. Some would argue that both life-sustaining treatment and what are considered forms of basic healthcare may only be withdrawn or withheld if death is imminent and inevitable. Such an approach ignores the exceptions contained in Pope John Paul II's teaching and would seem to disregard both the idea of burden for the non-terminal patient and also hundreds of years of Catholic theological thought. Can we presume that breathing always with the assistance of a respirator is never an excessive burden? Might not its continuance place a moral burden on the person, endangering his relationship with God?

40. Is the withdrawing of artificial nutrition and hydration from a persistently unconscious person a form of euthanasia?

Medical literature refers the condition of a patient who, due to some trauma, has suffered severe brain damage as being in a "persistent vegetative state." This is an awkward term because such people do not become vegetables. Medically this state means that the cerebral cortex of the brain has been severely damaged and does not function as it once did, while the brain stem—which regulates the body temperature, breathing, and heartbeat—continues to function. A thorny question arises regarding this condition, namely, must artificial nutrition and hydration always be given to such patients? It is a difficult question because it asks if such nutrition and hydration in these situations are extraordinary means of preserving life or simply always basic healthcare.

In 2004, Pope John Paul II addressed this question. He said the person in the vegetative state has a right to basic healthcare that includes cleanliness, warmth, nutrition, and hydration. To be more precise, he states that the administration of such nutrition and hydration by artificial means is not a medical act but a natural means of preserving life. Such nutrition and hydration should be considered, in principle, ordinary and proportionate means to preserve life and be morally obligatory, as long as it does what it is supposed to do. The pope describes its purpose as providing nourishment to the patient and alleviating suffering.

One might think that such a statement would end the debate on this issue. Commentators point out, however, that by using the words, "in principle," the pope allows for exceptions. In other words, there could be cases where such provision of artificial nutrition and hydration could be judged to be a burden to the patient and could actually exceed the benefit to the patient. For example, the Australian Bishop's Conference in 2004 acknowledged that "in particular cases, however, the provision of nutrition and hydration may cease to be obligatory, e.g., if the patient is unable to assimilate the material provided or if the manner of the provision itself causes undue suffering to the patient, or involves an undue burden to others. As the Catholic Health Australia Code notes, in Australia tube feeding is not normally too burdensome to others" (Briefing Note on the Obligation to Provide Nutrition and Hydration, #3).

Other commentators interpret the pope's words, "in principle," differently. They stress that no one can predict who will recover from such a coma, and since there is always hope of recovery, one should supply artificial nutrition and hydration unless the patient is clearly in the dying process. This opinion exceeds the teaching of John Paul II and the Congregation for the Doctrine of the Faith and may, in itself, place an excessive burden on a patient or a family. The teaching is clear that nutrition and hydration should be provided as long as they fulfill their function. If they do not, they may legitimately be withdrawn, whether a patient is dying or not. The abstract hope for future medical knowledge is not a justification for ignoring the failure of nutrition and hydration to fulfill its purpose for the ill patient before our eyes.

41. Is it wrong for the Christian to fear death?

Life is a gift from God, while death is unavoidable. We might readily accept that life is a gift from God but wonder why death is unavoidable. In 1944, Pope Pius XII reflected that God had not wished to include suffering and death in our destiny but through one man sin entered the world and with sin came death. It remains a mystery to us precisely how the misuse of our freedom from the beginning introduced suffering and death to our human destiny. Yet, as people of faith, we can see death in a new light because of the life, death, and resurrection of Christ. Death does not just end earthly life but brings it to fulfillment in the resurrection.

Saying and believing these spiritual reflections on death does not necessarily get rid of an underlying fear of death. Death is a mysterious and unknown road to us and can be accompanied by pain and suffering and the dread of partings. Despite reflection on death and even given circumstances that may psychologically prepare us for death, such as prolonged illness, advanced age, and recurring suffering, "nevertheless the fact remains that death…is something which naturally causes people anguish." (*Declaration on Euthanasia*, section III.)

This is why we need others to help us deal with the fear of death and to assist us to die with dignity. Throughout the history of the Church, spiritual writers have reflected on death, and the faithful have been encouraged to pray for and prepare for a peaceful death. Even though many of us are now in an age and a culture of longer lives and greater cures, we will all have to confront the fears, denial, anger, and acceptance that can be linked to the dying process. This holds true for the dying person, health professionals, pastoral care workers, family, and friends of the dying. To be able to come through what might be a frightening process of dying is one of the great moments of growth in the human life cycle. In order for death to be such a moment we will need to confirm our trust in the mercy of God to be greater than all our sins and limitations, and we will hopefully be accompanied by people of compassion and faith helping us to gently open the door to eternal life.

42. Is it all right to want to die?

This is an ambiguous question, for it could refer to someone who is in the dying process or it could refer to a person in good physical health. Popular psychological writings on death and dying often list the five different stages that people might go through when they are dying, namely: denial, anger, bargaining, depression, and acceptance. For Christians the last stage of acceptance is saying "yes" to God's will. They may have been reconciled to God and others, said the things they have wanted to say, finished any unfinished business, and feel ready to leave this world and return to God. For the dying person with faith, there may come a time when the desire to be fully united to her loving God takes priority over all other concerns and she actually desires to die. Her eyes turn toward the next life and she is not only ready to go but desires to go. This desire to leave this life is not the result of despair but rather the fruit of Christian hope.

We have a different situation when someone is not dying or is in good physical health, for the desire to die may indicate desperation or depression rather than acceptance and hope. Such persons may need personal and professional help to regain a zest for the life God has given them until the time comes that God calls them to himself.

43. How do we know that a person is really dead?

From a purely biological perspective, we can say that a person is dead when there are signs that his unifying life functions have ceased. In the past such key signs would have been the stopping of the heart and the cessation of the breathing function. People of faith would interpret death as a more complex and mysterious reality than the mere biological, because when unifying life functions cease it means that the spiritual principle of the person, or his soul, will soon leave the earthly body.

Because of advances in medicine, new questions have arisen regarding the definition of death. Machines can now aid the function of the heart and the lungs even after such functions have naturally ceased. So we could have the situation where a patient's heart and lungs are functioning with the aid of machines but he is in fact already dead because the entire brain, including the brain stem, has totally ceased to function; this is called "brain death." So while in most cases the cessation of the cardiopulmonary functions is a sign of death, there are more complex cases where a person may be on a respirator but we are not sure if he is alive or dead. The criteria for brain death are employed in such cases.

There is a range of tests to determine brain death, including: testing for reflexes in the brain stem, testing for cerebral functions, and even detecting blood flow or lack of blood flow in the brain. The Uniform Determination of Death Act (UDDA) states: "An individual who has sustained either (1) irreversible cessation of circulatory and respiratory functions, or (2) irreversible cessation of all functions of the entire brain including the brain stem, is dead" (Uniform Determination of Death Act, page 3). The phrase "all functions of the entire brain" is important because a person in the PVS or permanently comatose state can have a functioning brain stem, all or partially preserved hypothalamic function, and minimal brain activity. The person may be able to breathe unaided by a machine. Such a person is not dead.

Not only has the issue of PVS and coma patients raised questions about the definition of death. With the possibility of organ transplants now and with the knowledge that such transplants have a better chance of success if organs are harvested from a body which still has blood flow, we need to be sure that people have actually died before their organs are harvested (see question #18 in the life "In Between" section). So while the traditional signs of death or the cessation of the unifying life principles are most commonly used to determine death, there are situations where the determination that the whole of the brain is dead is deemed necessary. The Christian believes that while our earthly body dies, it will be raised to a new life in heaven. For the person of faith, life is not ended in death, but changed.

44. Why think about death now?

In times when life was more precarious and the average life span was much shorter, it should not be surprising that a range of spiritualities within the Catholic tradition promoted frequent reflection on death. For example, Saint Alphonsus Liguori wrote a work titled *Preparation for Death*, which consisted of a series of stories coupled with spiritual advice so that the person of faith could die well and be prepared to face the judgment of God. Spiritual books dealing with the art of dying were once common to prepare clergy to assist the dying faithful.

Even though fewer sermons and spiritual works deal directly with death and dying today—and the majority of publications in this area usually deal with the psychological aspects of the dying process—the Christian is well served to reflect on and pray about this inescapable human experience. In fact, there comes a time when circumstances give us an opportunity for such prayer and reflection, namely, when we are confronted with the dying of another, a relative, or friend. Such intense experiences usually encourage us to ask the big questions about life. These questions may include: What is really important in my life? Do I have my priorities right? Do I see my own troubles in a proper perspective? On whom can I really rely? What does my faith mean to me, and am I ready to stand before God?

If we have thought and prayed about death we will also be in a better position to assist those who are dying. If we have always kept death as a stranger at the door of our consciousness and prayer life, how prepared will we be to talk about death with a friend or relative who needs such an intimate exchange? Our own fear of death can deprive another of coming to terms with death.

We have to deal with "little deaths" every day. These little deaths may include disappointments, betrayals, relationship breakdowns, financial loss. How we negotiate our way through these experiences with prayer and reflection will in the long run help us to deal with the realities of denial, sorrow, anger, and acceptance that may be part of our final stages of life. Also, thinking about death now may encourage us to make decisions about advance medical directives. For the person of faith, thinking about death is not meant to be a morbid or obsessive preoccupation, rather, it is simply a way to affirm that if we live, we live for the Lord, and when we die, we will die for the same Lord.

45. Why should we show respect for a corpse?

There is a common misunderstanding that sometime after we die our soul leaves our body and goes on to eternal life and has nothing to do with the body again. It is true that death marks the end of the earthly body, but at the resurrection we will have resurrected bodies united with our souls. We state this each time we pray the Nicene Creed.

Even though our dead earthly body could be described as just a mass of organic matter that will eventually decompose like any other dead body, we show it particular respect in our manner of acting and in the use of rituals. Respect for this dead earthly body reveals or symbolizes the reverence with which we held the person who was once associated with this body. In other words, our reverence for the dead body expresses our reverence for the life of this particular person, for human life in general, and for the Creator of all life. Signs of respect for the corpse also acknowledge that the person we once knew and loved will be whole again at the resurrection of the dead.

The presence of the body at a liturgical service can enable people to grieve, to pray, to say goodbye, to express the depth of their love for the deceased, and to feel support from family, friends, and the community of faith. We are symbolic people, and the dead body is rich in symbolism for the living, especially for the living faithful. The corpse and the respect we show it is really declaring that if such an earthly body receives so much reverence, then how wonderful must be those who in their resurrected body enjoy eternal life.

Such practices as autopsy and organ donation, if performed correctly, do not show any signs of disrespect for the dead earthly body. In fact such practices can be for the good of others. An autopsy could reveal the cause of death and may advance scientific knowledge, or it could even lead to the apprehension of one who has had no respect for human life and caused the death of another. People can make a gift of their body to science or choose to be an organ donor. The donation of organs, far from being seen as mutilation or disrespectful of the body, has been described by John Paul II as a great gift of charity.

46. Why can Catholics now be cremated when this practice was once not allowed?

Believing that our body is the temple of the Holy Spirit and that we will share in the resurrection of Christ, the Catholic

Church has practiced burial of the dead since the very early days of the Church. For the early Christians, cremation was viewed as a pagan practice, since pagan Rome at the beginning of the Christian era used to burn the bodies of the dead. Christians, on the other hand, adhered to the ancient custom of the Jews and the more ancient custom of earlier Romans of burying the dead in the ground. Cremation was seen as a symbolic means of denying the resurrection of the body and asserting that death was the total annihilation of the human person.

Of course, cremation in itself does not have to carry such a meaning, namely, the denial of the immortality of the soul and the resurrection of the body. The body in the earth eventually returns to dust just as the cremated body turns to ashes. The Church in the past actually allowed the cremation of bodies during times of epidemic.

With a decrease in the number of organizations and societies that employed cremation as a means of denying the Christian truths about resurrection, the Holy Office (now known as the Congregation for the Doctrine of the Faith) abrogated the ban on cremation in 1969. Prayers and rituals were to take place in the presence of the body, and cremation was allowed to follow afterward.

With the revised funeral rites, *Ordo Exsequiarum,* which followed the Second Vatican Council, allowance was made for the Committal Rite to take place at the graveside or the crematorium. Normally the actual funeral Mass would be celebrated in the presence of the body, and the Committal Rite would take place at the crematorium. While allowing for such practice to continue, the 1983 revised *Code of Canon Law* continued to stress the traditional preference for burying of the dead but clearly stated that the Church "does not, however, forbid cremation unless it has been chosen for reasons which are contrary to Catholic teaching" (*Canon* 1176).

47. Can you have a funeral Mass in the presence of cremated remains?

The *Order of Christian Funerals*, in use in the Catholic Church since 1989, outlines three separate rites to celebrate Christian death and entry into the next life. First, there is the vigil of prayers, which is held before the funeral Mass, then the funeral Mass itself, and finally the Rite of Committal, which takes place at the graveside or the crematorium.

Normally, for the person who has chosen to be cremated, there would be the vigil, the funeral Mass in the presence of the body, and then the Committal Rite at the crematorium. This order, however, created problems for some families. What of a loved one who died in another country and the cost of returning the body went beyond the family's means? What if the deceased had donated his body to science and only sometime later the family received the cremated remains? One solution was to reverse the order of the rites, that is, have the Rite of Committal at the crematorium first and then, at a later date, have a memorial Mass for the deceased. The *Order of Christian Funerals* states that if cremation has been chosen, then the funeral Mass was not to take place in the presence of the cremated remains.

The U.S. bishops, aware of the pastoral needs of their people, namely, that some families felt the need in certain circumstances to have a funeral Mass celebrated in the presence of the cremated remains of their loved one, asked Rome for permission to allow the funeral Mass to be celebrated in the presence of a person's ashes. So in 1997, the Holy See granted permission to the U.S. bishops to allow funeral Masses in the presence of cremated remains.

Although there are some minor changes in some of the wording of the prayers to acknowledge that there are cremated remains and not a body, the funeral Mass is celebrated as it is with the body of the deceased present. In this way, if cremation is chosen for the proper reasons, the Church can express its love and compassion for the faithful who mourn and honor their departed brothers and sisters in the hope of the resurrection.

48. Can I have Catholic rites for a miscarried baby?

A book of blessings prepared by the International Commission on English in the Liturgy states: "In times of death and grief the Christian turns to the Lord for consolation and strength. This is especially true when a child dies before birth. This blessing is provided to assist the parents in their grief and console them with the blessing of God" (*Book of Blessings*, prepared by International Commission on English in the Liturgy, a Joint Commission of Catholic Bishops' Conferences, 1989, #279). The book then supplies a selection of blessings, petitions, and prayers for the deceased and for the parents of the deceased. This practice seems most fitting because the Church teaches that human life begins at conception and states that even though the baby may not have been baptized, if the parents intended to baptize their baby, there may be a Catholic funeral (*Canon* 1183.2).

Many families may opt to pray for the deceased baby, especially in cases of early miscarriage, rather than have a formal burial according to Catholic rites. This is so because the remains may be minimal. Of course the different ways of dealing with such a tragic death and laying the remains to rest do not detract from the fact that human life is sacred from the moment of conception (*Catechism*, Nos. 2270–75). The Church prays for the souls of miscarried and aborted babies, and commends them to the mercy of God (*Catechism*, No. 1261).

Many people who work in pastoral care suggest that some ritual or ceremony be used to deal with the loss of a baby by miscarriage. The cost of a funeral may be prohibitive for some or too emotionally traumatic for others, but there are other ceremonies that can help with the healing of the parents such as naming the child, writing out one's now-lost hopes for this child, joining with chosen family and friends to acknowledge the loss. While the Church often overlooked the ritualizing of the loss through miscarriage, our modern society has lost much of its sense of ritual as a way of dealing with loss—to the detriment of those who are expected to carry on as if nothing happened.

49. The priest has come to anoint my sick grandfather. The priest said this was a "sacrament of healing," but he is not getting better. Why does the Church call this a sacrament of healing?

While it is true that the revision to the Roman Rite of the anointing of the sick in 1972 puts greater stress than in the preceding centuries on the healing aspect of the sacrament, we need to consider the wide range of effects flowing from the grace of this sacrament and understand healing in all its many dimensions.

The anointing of the sick can bring both spiritual and physical strength during an illness and even approaching death. For this sacrament conveys several graces and imparts healing and strengthening in the Holy Spirit against anxiety, discouragement, temptation, and gives peace and fortitude (CCC 1520). These graces flow from the atoning death of Jesus Christ, for "he took our infirmities and bore our diseases" (Matthew 8:17).

The *Catholic Catechism* lists the effects of the sacrament as follows: "The special grace of the sacrament of the anointing of the sick has as its effects: the uniting of the sick person to the passion of Christ, for his own good and that of the whole Church; the strengthening, peace, and courage to endure in a Christian manner the sufferings of illness or old age; the forgiveness of sins, if the sick person was not able to obtain it through the sacrament of penance; the restoration of health, if it is conducive to the salvation of his soul; the preparation for passing to eternal life" (CCC 1532).

People often ask why healing of the body happens only in some cases and not in others. We should avoid extreme responses. Some may argue that if a Christian is not physically healed in the sacrament, then this reflects a lack of faith on her part. This is a simplistic response. God does not always heal us physically, even if we have strong faith, because all of God's graces, including physical health, are bestowed to lead to our salvation. Mysteriously, sometimes our salvation involves the lack of physical healing. This truth does not deny that God can physically heal us through the grace of the sacrament. The Catholic Church teaches that the sacrament brings "the restoration of health, if it is conducive to the salvation of his soul" (CCC 1532).

Therefore, if our grandfather is anointed and is not physically healed, we can still trust that God's healing power is at work and we can still say that the sacrament is truly healing.

50. When the priest arrived at the hospital, my wife had already died. Why did he refuse to anoint her? She was a good Catholic.

The death of a spouse or of any loved one is painful enough and may be made even worse by any apparent insensitivity on the part of pastoral caregivers, especially a priest. Yet, the priest acted correctly in not anointing the woman who had already died. This question shows the need for good pastoral practice in terms of sensitivity to family members of the deceased and good catechesis regarding the celebration of the sacrament of the anointing of the sick.

Sound pastoral practice would move the priest to appropriate expressions of sympathy to a spouse and family members while inviting them to pray the Prayers for the Dead, as contained in the ritual, *Pastoral Care for the Sick*. This small ritual contains a variety of rites and prayers to respond to different situations. There are rituals for the sick, for the dying, and prayers for the deceased. The ritual addresses this particular situation when it says: "It may be necessary to explain to the family of the person who is dead that sacraments are celebrated for the living, not the dead, and that the dead are effectively helped by the prayers of the living" (#224).

Since the man's spouse has died, the ritual of anointing should not be celebrated. As we have suggested, however, that does not mean that no pastoral care can be given at this time. Rather, asking family and friends to pray for the deceased and to pray for themselves in their own grief is pastorally effective and uses the fitting prayers from the ritual. It even allows for adaptation. For example, the priest might ask those present to extend their hands in blessing over the deceased.

Good catechesis about this sacrament might be helpful to ward off misunderstandings about the conditions under which the various rituals should be celebrated. It might also serve to invite the broader Church community to hold the sick in prayer and even to foster more communal celebrations of the sacrament, reminding us of our responsibility to pray for those who are sick, in need of healing, as well as for those who have died.

SOURCES FOR FURTHER READING

Sources from the Vatican

The following sources are available on the Vatican website: vatican.va

Catechism of the Catholic Church.

Code of Canon Law.

John XXIII. Peace on Earth *(Pacem in Terris)*. Encyclical letter. April 11, 1963.

John Paul II. The Gospel of Life *(Evangelium vitae)*. Encyclical letter. March 25, 1995.

John Paul II. On the Christian Meaning of Human Suffering *(Salvifici doloris)*. February 11, 1984.

John Paul II. The Splendor of Truth *(Veritatis splendor)*. Encyclical letter. August 1, 1993.

John Paul II. "To the participants in the International Congress on 'Life-Sustaining Treatments and Vegetative State: Scientific Advances and Ethical Dilemmas.'" March 20, 2004.

John Paul II. Speech to the personnel of the Nuova Regina Margherita Hospital. December 20, 1981 (only available in Italian and Portuguese).

Pontifical Academy for Life. *Declaration on the Production and the Scientific and Therapeutic Use of Human Embryonic Stem Cells.* August 25, 2000.

Pontifical Council for Pastoral Assistance to Health Care Workers. *The Charter for Healthcare Workers.* 1995. Available from the Vatican; full text not online.

Sacred Congregation for the Doctrine of the Faith. *Declaration on Euthanasia.* May 5, 1980.

Sacred Congregation for the Doctrine of the Faith. *Declaration on Procured Abortion.* November 18, 1974.

Sacred Congregation for the Doctrine of the Faith. *Instruction* Dignitas Personae *on Certain Bioethical Questions.* June 20, 2008.

Sacred Congregation for the Doctrine of the Faith. *Instruction on Respect for Human Life in its Origin and on the Dignity of Procreation. Replies to Certain Questions of the Day (*Donum vitae*).* February 22, 1987.

Sacred Congregation for the Doctrine of the Faith. *Responses to Certain Questions of the United States Conference of Catholic Bishops Concerning Artificial Nutrition and Hydration.* August 1, 2007, and "Commentary" on *Responses to Certain Questions of the United States Conference of Catholic Bishops Concerning Artificial Nutrition and Hydration.*

Sacred Congregation for Divine Worship and the Discipline of the Sacraments, letter of March 21, 1997, permitting individual U.S. diocesan bishops to decide whether to allow cremated remains of a body to be present at the funeral Mass (available at usccb.org/liturgy/current/cremation.shtml).

Sources from Conferences of Bishops

Australian Bishops Committee for Doctrine and Morals/Bishops Committee for Healthcare/Catholic Health Australia. *Briefing Note on the Obligation to Provide Nutrition and Hydration,* 2004.

United States Conference of Catholic Bishops. *Ethical and Religious Directives for Catholic Healthcare Services.* Fifth edition. November 17, 2009.

Other Sources

Saint Alphonsus Liguori. *Preparation for Death.*

Ashley, Benedict; DeBlois, Jean; and O'Rourke, Kevin. *Health Care Ethics: A Catholic Theological Analysis.* Fifth Edition. Washington, D.C.: Georgetown University Press, 2006.

International Commission on English in the Liturgy, a Joint Commission of Catholic Bishops' Conferences. *Book of Blessings.* Collegeville, MN: The Liturgical Press, 1989.

National Conference of Commissioners on Uniform State Laws. *The Uniform Determination of Death Act.* Chicago, IL: 1980

O'Neil, Kevin, and Black, Peter. *The Essential Moral Handbook.* Revised edition. Liguori, MO: Liguori Publications, 2006.

Order of Christian Funerals With Cremation Rite. New York: Catholic Book Publishing Company.

Pastoral Care of the Sick. Rites of Anointing and Viaticum. New York: Catholic Book Publishing Company.

Handbook for Today's Catholic
Revised Edition

ISBN 978-0-7648-1220-0

Handbook for Today's Catholic is presented in easy-to-understand language, with content divided into beliefs, practices, prayers, and living the faith, and is also fully indexed to the *Catechism of the Catholic Church*. RCIA and parish adult faith formation groups, high school religious education classes, inquirers into the Catholic faith, and anyone who wants to have the essentials of Catholicism at their fingertips will welcome this affordable faith resource.

How Can I Find God?
The Famous and the Not-So-Famous Consider the Quintessential Question
James Martin

ISBN 978-0-7648-0090-0

This vibrant collection brings together an array of voices addressing the question of how one might approach the search for God. With contributors from many faith traditions, this book will be of value to all who are seeking to answer the question, "How Can I Find God?"

Living the Ten Commandments as a Catholic Today
Compiled by: Mathew J. Kessler

ISBN 978-0-7648-1849-3

Living the Ten Commandments as a Catholic today is written to "open up" the commandments and make them understandable and relevant for our lives today. Their messages are timeless—tell the truth, respect your parents, don't commit adultery—but it's hard sometimes to put their meaning into the context of today's hectic, fast-paced world. This book provides an additional meditation to the originally published articles that bring home the message of the commandments. With questions after each chapter, this book would be perfect for small-group discussions or personal reflection.

CPSIA information can be obtained
at www.ICGtesting.com
Printed in the USA
LVOW13s0333220917
549616LV00008B/76/P